#7

D1265625

GLOBAL ORGANIZATIONS

The Organization of the Petroleum Exporting Countries

GLOBAL ORGANIZATIONS

The African Union

The Arab League

The Association of Southeast Asian Nations

The Caribbean Community

The European Union

The International Atomic Energy Agency

The Organization of American States

The Organization of the Petroleum
Exporting Countries

The United Nations

The United Nations Children's Fund

The World Bank and
the International Monetary Fund

The World Health Organization

The World Trade Organization

GLOBAL ORGANIZATIONS

The Organization of the Petroleum Exporting Countries

Heather Lehr Wagner

Series Editor
Peggy Kahn
University of Michigan–Flint

CHELSEA HOUSE
PUBLISHERS
An imprint of Infobase Publishing

The Organization of the Petroleum Exporting Countries

Copyright © 2009 by Infobase Publishing

Chelsea House
An imprint of Infobase Publishing
132 West 31st Street
New York NY 10001

Library of Congress Cataloging-in-Publication Data
Wagner, Heather Lehr.
  The Organization of the Petroleum Exporting Countries / by Heather Lehr Wagner.
      p. cm. — (Global organizations)
Includes bibliographical references and index.
ISBN 978-1-60413-102-4 (hardcover)
1. Organization of Petroleum Exporting Countries. 2. Petroleum industry and trade.
I. Title. II. Series.

HD9560.5.W233 2008
382'.42282—dc22   2008020546

Chelsea House books are available at special discounts when purchased in bulk quantities for businesses, associations, institutions, or sales promotions. Please call our Special Sales Department in New York at (212) 967-8800 or (800) 322-8755.

You can find Chelsea House on the World Wide Web at http://www.chelseahouse.com

Series design by Erik Lindstrom
Cover design by Ben Peterson

Printed in the United States of America

Bang KT 10 9 8 7 6 5 4 3 2 1

This book is printed on acid-free paper.

All links and Web addresses were checked and verified to be correct at the time of publication. Because of the dynamic nature of the Web, some addresses and links may have changed since publication and may no longer be valid.

CONTENTS

INTRODUCTION

A Reformer's Plan

IN 1960, THE NEWLY APPOINTED DIRECTOR-GENERAL OF petroleum and mineral affairs in Saudi Arabia had little patience for the "special relationship" that members of the Saudi royal family had sought to develop with the United States. It was a relationship based almost exclusively on oil—a relationship that he, forty-two-year-old Abdullah Tariki, believed did little to benefit Saudi Arabia.

For several decades, since the beginning of the twentieth century, in fact—as the value of oil had been slowly recognized—the major global powers (Great Britain, Germany, the Netherlands, France, and the United States) had moved throughout the Middle East claiming oil wherever it could be found. They did this by sending representatives to negotiate exclusive rights to oil, known as concessions—the rights to hunt for oil and ultimately manage any oil that was discovered—with the ruling powers in that region of the world.

The first major oil concession was secured by the British in 1901, when William Knox D'Arcy won an agreement in Persia (now Iran) for what would become the Anglo-Persian Oil Company. The British government was a majority owner, and the company remained exclusively British until 1954. During the first decade of the twentieth century, the competition for oil concessions also focused on Iraq, where British, German, Dutch, and American companies were all eager to win concessions. Ultimately, the three European powers banded together and won the right to Iraq's oil supply. The result was the Turkish Petroleum Company (Iraq at the time was part of the Ottoman Empire and was ruled from Turkey), but it was Turkish in name only, as the British controlled 50 percent of the company, with Dutch and German interests each controlling 25 percent. After World War I (1914–1918), the German rights were transferred to France to create what would become known as the Iraq Petroleum Company, while the United States demanded and was given half of the British share.

The United States increased its share again in 1930, when a U.S. oil company, Standard Oil Company of California (Socal) won full rights to the Bahrain concession, even though Bahrain was a British protectorate. Three years later, Socal also narrowly outmaneuvered British oil companies to gain the concession in Saudi Arabia.

The United States ultimately emerged as the major winner of oil concessions in the Middle East. Through negotiations, treaties, and intense and fiery lobbying, the Americans won 100 percent of the oil resources in Saudi Arabia and Bahrain, 50 percent in Kuwait, 40 percent in Iran, and 25 percent in Iraq.[1]

A KINGDOM IN DISARRAY

This overwhelming amount of American control over oil in the Middle East—particularly in Saudi Arabia—was troubling Tariki as he assumed the post of director-general of petroleum and mineral affairs, or "oil minister." The Americans, he believed, had far too much control over a Saudi resource, and the Saudi royal family seemed unwilling or unable to change that fact.

Located in the southern portion of the Middle East, Saudi Arabia stretches over a territory as vast as western Europe. From the time of its establishment in 1932, when the founder of the Saudi dynasty—Abdul Aziz al-Saud (known commonly in the West as "Ibn Saud")—completed the unification of several Arab kingdoms under his rule, Saudi Arabia has been under the strict control of the Saudi royal family. The descendants of Ibn Saud have enjoyed absolute rule, in that all major decisions governing the kingdom are made by members of the royal family. Upon the death of one king, members of the family gather to determine which one of them is best suited to serve as the new ruler.

Tariki was a reformer, inspired by the pro-Arab policies of Egypt's leader, Gamal Abdel Nasser, who argued that Arab nations in the Middle East should not be governed by foreign occupiers or royal families but instead by a system that guaranteed the lands belonged to the people who lived there. Tariki had been educated in Kuwait and Egypt and had more recently been motivated by Nasser's focus on promoting social and economic reforms, development, and anticolonialism. Nasser's fiery speeches targeted monarchies in the region—particularly Iraq, Jordan, and Saudi Arabia—that maintained strong ties with, and in some cases owed their thrones to, the Western powers.

Tariki was viewed with some suspicion by the Saudi royal family, especially Tariki's onetime mentor, Prince Faisal. Faisal worried that Tariki would create trouble in an industry

Abdullah Tariki, appointed oil minister of Saudi Arabia in 1960, was determined to ensure greater Saudi control over its oil resources.

dependent on the West and add to recent strains in the relationship between the United States and Saudi Arabia.

Faisal understood the West, especially the United States, as few other members of the Saudi royal family did. From the time he was 14 years old, he had represented his popular father, Ibn Saud, spending time in Europe and the United States as his father's personal envoy. He also earned a degree in petroleum engineering from the University of Texas in the 1940s, before going to work in the Saudi Arabian Finance Ministry. He was hardworking, sophisticated, and had a clear vision for his country.

Unfortunately, Faisal did not inherit the Saudi throne upon his father's death. Instead, his older half-brother Saud became king. Saud had none of Faisal's shrewdness or understanding of economics and foreign policy; he plundered the Saudi treasury to build lavish palaces for himself; and he tried to form an alliance with Egypt's Nasser. When that alliance failed, he was implicated in a plot to have Nasser assassinated. In 1958, the members of the Saudi royal family persuaded Saud to turn all real power for running the kingdom over to Faisal, but by 1960, Saud had regained control of the monarchy.

It was in this unstable time that Tariki became oil minister. He saw that Saud was failing to assert sufficient control over Saudi oil and believed that the Americans would exploit it with no thought to Saudi interests. He also felt that the companies paid Saudi Arabia royalties far below the value of the oil they controlled. In response, Tariki was determined to ensure greater Saudi control over its oil resources and to win Saudi independence from the American oil company that had won the Saudi concession, which was by then known as Aramco, the Arabian American Oil Company.

ARAMCO

Despite its name, Aramco was, in its early days, a joint venture between two American oil companies, Socal and Texaco. The vast wealth of the Saudi reserves had presented Aramco with several problems. First, a great market awaited the oil in Europe, but to get it there a pipeline was needed to cross the desert to the Mediterranean, a project that would cost some $100 million. Second, refining the oil and promoting it to potential buyers would be expensive, and in the competitive market that existed, such costs mattered. Finally, officials with Aramco predicted that once the Saudis realized the extent and potential of their oil reserves, they would pressure Aramco to increase output—thereby increasing the amount of money the Saudi royal family received from the oil.

To help overcome these problems, Aramco invited two other oil companies to join their partnership. These companies were also American but they contributed not only financial resources but also international expertise and access to markets in Europe. Ultimately, Jersey Standard (formerly, Standard Oil of New Jersey and eventually Exxon) and Socony-Vacuum (formerly Standard Oil of New York, and eventually Mobil) also became partners in Aramco.

With the new partnership, Aramco's influence in Saudi Arabia grew in extraordinary quantities, largely because oil revenue formed the basis of Saud's wealth. As he spent more and more money on lavish new palaces and other luxuries, he became even more dependent on oil revenue, and less willing to alienate Aramco.

Saud and his half-brother Faisal agreed on few things, but in this area they were of one mind: Aramco should not be antagonized. Faisal knew that a cordial relationship with Aramco was key to a cordial relationship with the United States, and American assistance was valuable in both the defense of the kingdom and in preserving its standing in the global economy. Saudi Arabia, Faisal believed, did not yet have the ability to independently produce its own oil and distribute it around the world without the assistance of the United States. And he worried that the new oil minister was unnecessarily antagonistic. He told Tariki to "be reasonable and fair, and to protect not only Saudi Arabia's interests but also Aramco's."[2]

Tariki focused more on protecting Saudi Arabia's interests than protecting Aramco's. His skill was in using his charm to disarm his opponents, then speaking his mind bluntly. A reporter for *Petroleum Week* said of Tariki, "He [could] say the most drastic things with the most pleasant smile."[3]

In 1954, Tariki had promoted a deal with Aristotle Onassis, the Greek shipping tycoon, which would have switched the rights to transport Saudi oil from Aramco to Onassis's company. It took four years of intense legal battles in Saudi courts and, ultimately, the International Court of Justice before Aramco won the right to continue to ship Saudi oil. After that case was finally settled, Tariki argued that the Aramco concession should be renegotiated. His claim was that Saudi Arabia was simply a very young country when the concession had first been signed and had not then had the legal and political knowledge to protect its own interests.

OPEC IS FORMED

Tariki's arguments took on greater significance when Aramco decided to cut the price it paid for Saudi oil. A global surplus of oil had prompted the larger oil companies to dramatically reduce the prices they were charging for oil. These price reductions were made between February 1959 and August 1960, without any prior discussions or advance consultations with the oil-producing countries, and included a cut of 10 cents per barrel on August 8, 1960.

Now, a reduction of ten cents may seem small, but multiplied by the millions of barrels that were being pumped out of the Saudi oil reserves, the amount had a shattering economic impact on the Saudi kingdom. Tariki was furious at the action, and he used it to emphasize what he had been arguing—that Saudi Arabia could not be economically dependent on oil without having some control over its production, distribution, and pricing.

A year before he became oil minister, at a meeting of the Arab Petroleum Congress in Cairo, Egypt, Tariki quietly put out feelers with the representatives of other countries to see who would be interested in forming an organization to defend against oil company price-slashing. He found an ally in the Venezuelan minister of energy, Juan Pablo Pérez Alfonso, whose country also had large oil reserves being exploited by Shell, Standard Oil, and Gulf Oil. Pérez Alfonso shared the view that his country was not receiving a fair share from the oil companies, even though in the 1940s, he had negotiated the deal that gave Venezuela half of the profits those companies made from Venezuelan oil. He then urged other oil-producing states to negotiate similar arrangements.

The initial alliance between Pérez Alfonzo and Abdullah Tariki produced OPEC in 1960, an organization that began with only five members. In 2007, representatives from those original five countries joined nine additional members for an OPEC summit in Riyadh, Saudi Arabia. *Above, from left to right*, Sheikh Hamad bin Khalifa of Qatar, Sheikh Khalifa bin Zayed of the UAE, Iranian president Mahmoud Ahmadinejad, Venezuelan president Hugo Chavez, Saudi King Abdullah, Iraqi president Jalal Talabani, Indonesian vice-president Jusuf Kalla, Ecuadorian president Rafael Correa, and Nigerian president Umaru Yar'Adua.

In the 1950s, Pérez Alfonso lived for a time in the United States. He studied the early American experiments with oil exploration in Pennsylvania and, later, Texas. He saw how American oil barons like John Rockefeller had used deals with the railroads to limit oil distribution and manipulate profits. He returned to Venezuela heavily influenced by what he had learned about safeguarding Venezuela's resource from ruthless oil companies and convinced that the oil-producing nations needed to unite to maximize the income they could receive from oil. Soon, Pérez Alfonzo and Tariki had persuaded the representatives from Iran, Iraq, and Kuwait to draft recommendations to their governments to defend against the oil companies' pricing controls. No longer was a fifty-fifty split acceptable; instead the representatives wanted a sixty-forty split in their favor, as well as increased domestic refining capacity and more stable markets to protect their governments' revenue.

From September 10 to 14, 1960, representatives from Iran, Iraq, Kuwait, Saudi Arabia, and Venezuela gathered in Baghdad, Iraq. It was a simple beginning—12 men gathered in a small room around a table covered with a white cloth and a phone on a chair—but by the time the meeting concluded, the Organization of the Petroleum Exporting Countries (OPEC) had been formed. Its goal was to defend the price of oil and eliminate price fluctuations with "due regard being given at all times to the interests of oil-producing nations and to the necessity of securing a steady income for them."[4]

Tariki's criticism of Aramco and the lack of Saudi control over its oil were interpreted as indirect criticism of the Saudi royal family and the relationship they had cultivated. By 1962, he was removed from his post by the increasingly powerful Prince Faisal and went into exile, traveling in Europe and in other parts of the Middle East before ultimately spending his last years of life in Cairo. He died there of a heart attack on September 7, 1997, at the age of 80.

Tariki never regained his political prominence. But he forever altered the relationship between oil companies and oil-producing countries. It would take OPEC several years to effectively organize, but the seeds planted by Tariki would blossom into an organization that could use oil not only as a resource but also as a powerful tool to ensure global influence.

The Oil Market

IN *OIL: ANATOMY OF AN INDUSTRY*, AUTHOR MATTHEW Yeomans decided to try an experiment: to spend a day without using oil. But the task proved far more challenging than simply not using his car. He could not use his shampoo, shaving cream, or deodorant (all oil-based products), or even his plastic shower curtain. His toothpaste contained a petrochemical- (or oil-) enhanced artificial coloring and mineral oils. Both his contact lenses and plastic-lens eyeglasses came from chemicals made using oil. He could not put disposable diapers on his six-month-old son. He could not wear his rubber-soled sneakers, nor put on waterproof outerwear when he went out into the rain. The streets in his New York neighborhood were paved with asphalt, which is a by-product of the process of refining crude oil to extract gasoline and heating oil. He could not make eggs in a nonstick pan, or prepare coffee in a heat-resistant glass pot. Nor could he use credit or debit cards (oil-based plastic) to pay for any purchases. The computer and telephone were off-limits, as both were cased in plastic. CDs and DVDs were also banned. The list was seemingly endless—bandages, garbage bags, glue, even aspirin![5]

Oil plays a vital role in daily American life, sometimes in visible ways and sometimes in ways that are more obscure. Oil is the key to transportation, providing fuel for vehicles and airplanes. More than half of the oil consumed daily in the United States—and one barrel of every seven used in the world—is spent keeping American cars and trucks on the road.[6] Oil is also an important source of heat for homes in the winter. Oil contributes to the food supply, providing fuel to run farm and food-processing machinery. It plays a role in the manufacture of plastics, and in many chemical-based medicines.

THE PATH TO THE PUMP

Americans are most clearly aware of actions and decisions taken by OPEC when they see the price of gasoline rise. Yet few truly understand how oil travels from beneath the ground or below the sea in some distant country to the gas pump at their local gasoline station.

Crude oil—literally, basic petroleum (meaning "rock oil" or "oil from the earth")—is found in underground reservoirs. This crude oil was formed millions of years ago, when the remains of plants and animals living in the water gradually sank to the bottom of the ocean floor and were buried in layers of sand, silt, and mud that built up over them. The remains were buried deeper and deeper over the years, and heat and pressure were generated by the layers above. Gradually, heat and pressure turned these remains into a combination of hydrogen and carbon molecules that eventually transformed into crude oil.

The conditions that formed crude oil as well as the variety of plants and animals that became part of the process millions

This Aramco oil platform in the Persian Gulf houses workers and machinery needed to drill oil and produce oil and/or gas through wells in the ocean bed. After the oil is taken from the earth, it is refined into products like petroleum jelly, gasoline, and propane.

of years ago vary from region to region. That means the crude oil extracted from, say, Texas will be quite different from the crude oil found in Saudi Arabia and the Persian Gulf, and that from Venezuela will be different from that under Alaska's North Slope. Each type of oil has its own distinct components and each requires a specific kind of processing. Processing techniques also transform crude oil into different chemicals, for example, a variety of fuels, not only gasoline but also diesel and propane, and ingredients for other products.

An effort to trace the path of oil from its origination to a gasoline pump might begin atop an oil platform in the Persian

Gulf, just one place where crude oil is extracted from the earth. One Iranian oil site, for example, is marked by eight main platforms, some connected by catwalks over the water. Beneath these are 42 valves, 50 wells, and 11 drilling, production, and processing platforms. A 150-mile pipeline carries the oil back to land.[7] Other networks of underwater pipes carry the extracted crude oil from one spot to another in a complicated chain that involves pumps, separators, dehydrators, and turbines.

In the second part of its journey, the crude oil is placed on tankers and shipped to a refinery. At this point, the crude oil is still a mixture of carbon and hydrogen, sulfur, salts, nitrogen, and metals. Author Lisa Margonelli describes the refinery as

 ## THE FIGHT FOR OIL

In some parts of the Gulf, the oil platforms of one country are visible from another; even at night, they are marked by the orange and yellow flames of a gas flare. Oil can draw countries together—OPEC is a clear example—or can inspire them to war. More than half of the world's oil reserves are found in the Persian Gulf. Even before OPEC was formed, the countries that cluster around the Gulf were impacted by the presence of this valuable resource and the involvement foreign nations had taken in the region because of it. Oil has added to the conflicts between Shia and Sunni Muslims, between Kurds and the countries in which they live, between religious governments and monarchies. It has played a role in border disputes between Iraq and Kuwait, Iraq and Iran, Bahrain and Qatar, Qatar and Iran, Qatar and Saudi Arabia, Saudi Arabia and Oman, Iran and the United Arab Emirates (UAE), Oman and UAE, and Saudi Arabia and UAE. Land is valuable in the Middle East, but land with oil beneath it is priceless.

a "molecular butcher" who is assigned the task of taking the crude oil and shaping it into smaller, usable parts.[8] These parts must be separated by weight and then reshaped by catalysts, vacuums, re-formers, and compressors.

This separation of molecules creates the different grades of gasoline we see at a gas pump. The different grades—regular, high octane, etc.—are really different assortments of molecules. High-octane gas contains more of the longer carbon chains, which are more expensive to produce. High-octane gas is not really a better type of gasoline; it is simply a different variety, designed for use in a specific type of high-performance engine. These high-performance engines use more compression, and the higher-octane gas is designed to withstand this compression. Unless a car specifically states that high-octane gas should be used, there is no need for the average car owner to buy this more expensive grade.

Oil reaches the refinery by pipeline, then moves through fractionating towers that use boiling point as a way to sort the different hydrocarbon strings. There are different trays within the towers; the hydrocarbons enter as gases and then condense in the trays with the lightest molecules on top and the heaviest on the bottom. The hydrocarbons pass through more pipes. In the fluid catalytic cracker, steam, hydrogen and a catalyst break the long hydrocarbon chains into shorter gasoline molecules. Any leftover heavy molecules form a kind of sludge, which then travels to a machine known as the coker. This sludge is processed into chunks of black carbon, which may be purchased by nations like China to use as cheap fuel.

The process of combining and breaking down the carbon chains continues when the gasoline actually powers a vehicle; it is this that causes the form of pollution known as emissions. An average driver burning 581 gallons of gasoline a year will produce 77 pounds of hydrocarbons, 575 pounds of carbon monoxide, 38.2 pounds of nitrogen oxides, and 11,450 pounds of carbon dioxide.[9]

At the refinery, gasoline must be blended into the correct mix of molecules that meet air quality standards. Cheaper crude oil often contains higher amounts of sulfur, requiring greater amounts of processing. The oil comes from a variety of places—it might come from the Persian Gulf, Venezuela, or Alaska's North Slope. Each type of oil has its own distinct components and requires specific kinds of processing, helping to determine the price of the final product.

BRANDING THE GASOLINE

Once the oil has been refined, it travels to a pipeline depot. Until this point, no difference exists between the gasoline that will end up in a Shell station and the gasoline that is sold under any other brand name or gasoline that is sold under no name at all. The differences that distinguish one brand of gasoline from another are very small, and they do not enter the picture until the gasoline has reached the pipeline depot. (In fact, a single depot may receive gasoline from several different refineries.)

Also added here is ethanol. Ethanol is a cleaner-burning, higher-octane motor fuel that is produced from renewable sources, often corn or other crops. Ethanol is added to ensure that the gasoline meets federal clean air standards by decreasing harmful emissions and to help reduce the cost of the gas. The result of this "blend" is generally 10 percent ethanol to 90 percent unleaded gasoline—all cars can run on this blend.

After processing at the pipeline depot, the gasoline is loaded by hoses into tanker trucks that transport the gasoline to gas stations for sale. This is when consumers finally encounter a crude oil product and have to pay for it.

Several factors play a role in that price. The rising price of gasoline is not the result of some conspiracy or arbitrary policy set by OPEC. The price of gasoline reflects all of the complicated steps that are necessary in the process of creating it. Federal and state efforts to combat air pollution and greenhouse gases have also resulted in additional restrictions on the refinery process, the addition of certain substances to the gasoline, and changes in how and where gasoline can be stored. Other costs include the cost of research and investment in developing countries and the cost of a U.S. military presence to protect oil facilities. When the supply of oil is threatened—when violence erupts in an oil-producing region, when a ruler of an oil-producing region vows to prevent access to its markets, when OPEC announces a decision to cut back on production—prices rise. When supplies of the most easily accessible oil resources are exhausted and more complicated processes of extraction must be used, prices rise. When competition for oil increases—when more and more citizens in the rapidly growing economies of China and India acquire and drive cars—less oil is available for everyone, and prices rise.

OPEC's Early Years

FROM ITS FIRST MEETING IN BAGHDAD, IRAQ, IN SEPTEMBER 1960, the Organization of the Petroleum Exporting Countries (OPEC) has increased both in membership and in influence. Initially, OPEC focused on the pricing of oil; since 1982, the oil ministers of OPEC member nations also meet regularly to discuss crude oil production quotas—limits or restrictions on how much oil each member nation can produce.

The initial members—"Founder Members"—of OPEC were five countries from two regions of the world: Iran, Iraq, Kuwait, and Saudi Arabia from the Middle East, and Venezuela from South America. Other nations soon joined, representing not only the Middle East and South America, but also Africa and Southeast Asia. Qatar (Middle East) joined OPEC in 1961. In 1962, Libya (Africa) and Indonesia (Southeast Asia) joined.

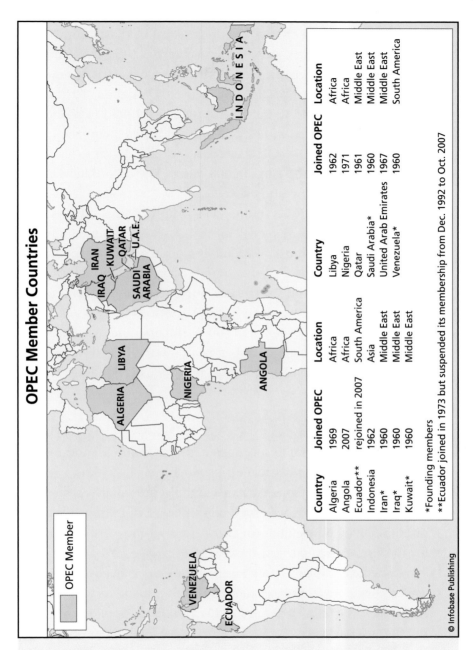

OPEC Member Countries

OPEC Member

Country	Joined OPEC	Location
Algeria	1969	Africa
Angola	2007	Africa
Ecuador**	rejoined in 2007	South America
Indonesia	1962	Asia
Iran*	1960	Middle East
Iraq*	1960	Middle East
Kuwait*	1960	Middle East

Country	Joined OPEC	Location
Libya	1962	Africa
Nigeria	1971	Africa
Qatar	1961	Middle East
Saudi Arabia*	1960	Middle East
United Arab Emirates	1967	Middle East
Venezuela*	1960	South America

*Founding members
**Ecuador joined in 1973 but suspended its membership from Dec. 1992 to Oct. 2007

© Infobase Publishing

OPEC was founded in 1960 by Saudi Arabia, Iran, Iraq, Kuwait, and Venezuela. Angola, which joined in 2007, is the newest member. In May 2008, Indonesia announced its withdrawal from the organization when its membership expires at the end of that year.

The United Arab Emirates, or UAE (Middle East), joined OPEC in 1967, and Algeria (Africa) joined in 1969. Nigeria (Africa) joined the organization in 1971. (Angola, Africa, is the most recent member, having joined in 2007. Gabon, Africa, was a member of OPEC, but it left in January 1995.) Ecuador, South America, joined in 1973, but suspended its membership from December 1992 to October 2007. Indonesia is set to leave the organization at the end of 2008 due to low oil production and lack of foreign investment.

According to OPEC's statute, "any country with a substantial net export of crude petroleum, which has fundamentally similar interests to those of Member Countries, may become a Full Member of the Organization, if accepted by a majority of three-fourths of Full Members, including the concurring votes of all Founder Members." OPEC specifies three types of members: Founder Members, Full Members, and Associate Members (an Associate Member is a country that does not qualify for full membership but may be admitted under special circumstances).

THE BEGINNING

At the beginning, OPEC struggled to maintain a cohesive policy. Each of the individual oil-producing states had its own specific policies. In some instances, the representatives they sent to OPEC were experienced oil ministers, but others were just as likely to be members of a royal family who were chosen for their relationship to the head of state.

Nonetheless, the oil companies were understandably wary at the time—the five countries that were OPEC's founders were the source of more than 80 percent of the world's crude oil exports. But the lack of expertise of the representatives and the sense that each country would ultimately focus only on its own best interests suggested that OPEC would be short-lived. Howard Page, a representative of Standard Oil, said of OPEC, "We attached little importance to it, because we believed it would not work."[10]

OPEC's achievements in its early years were limited. By its very formation, OPEC provided a kind of guarantee that oil companies would carefully consider any future plans for price cuts and would not take major steps without consulting the oil-producing countries first. But the contracts that had been negotiated years earlier and still remained in effect specified that the oil in the ground belonged to those who extracted it—the oil companies (with the exception of Iran, where a different agreement had been negotiated with a ruler friendly to Western interests).

In addition, in the 1960s, plenty of oil was available. The market was rich with oil supplies and new sources were being discovered. While the number of cars and other gasoline-consuming machines were increasing, as well, far more oil existed than these vehicles could consume. It was a competitive market in which the oil companies had to compete for buyers based upon price. The oil-producing nations were dependent on the revenue from oil and needed the companies to continue to market it for them.

International politics also played a role in those early years. King Faisal was in charge in Saudi Arabia; his Western-oriented policies ensured a kingdom that looked favorably upon the Western oil companies and sought to further develop its relationships with them. Venezuela was also eager to establish stronger ties with the United States, and the ruling shah of Iran had established a close alliance with American policymakers.

While the oil companies publicly declared their support for OPEC, they quietly worked behind the scenes to spark rivalries among the various member nations and negotiate separate deals with them. Numerous territorial disputes made those efforts easier. Kuwait gained its independence from Great Britain in 1961 and was immediately threatened with invasion by Iraq, which claimed that the Kuwaiti territory belonged to it. Great Britain was forced to offer military support to ensure

Kuwaiti independence, at which point Iraq ended its military campaign but also temporarily left OPEC in protest.

The shah of Iran, in particular, resisted many of OPEC's plans. His focus was on increasing his country's revenue from oil. He did not want to hold back production or raise prices—he wanted to sell more oil. "Iran must be restored to number one producer," he said. "International oil prorationing is nice in theory but unrealistic in practice."[11]

This was in direct conflict with OPEC's stated aims. From the beginning, the focus of OPEC was to stabilize oil prices and begin a process of "prorationing"—distributing oil production and revenues proportionally among the OPEC members.

In their very first conference, the OPEC members stated that they would "devise ways and means of ensuring the stabilization of prices in the international oil markets" to avoid "harmful and unnecessary fluctuations." They also stated that future price changes would happen only after prior consultation with oil-producing states. Finally, the first meeting had noted that, if an oil company attempted to penalize a country for actions taken by OPEC, then the other countries would not accept any better deals with that oil company.[12]

GLOBAL COMPETITION

Negotiating with the companies and controlling prices was not simply a matter of ensuring that the member countries fell in line and worked together, negotiating as a united front. Other countries were entering the oil market, offering the oil companies new sources for the valuable commodity and challenging any OPEC-member efforts to raise prices and increase revenue.

Eventually, many of these new oil-producing countries would become members of OPEC, but in the 1960s they were instead competitors, adding their oil to an already glutted market. Africa was a target for exploration, particularly by the French (since the Middle East was so heavily dominated by British and American oil companies), after oil was discovered in 1956 by a French company in France's North African colony of Algeria. The extraction process was a challenging one—the oil had been found deep under the Sahara desert and, only two years after its discovery, Algeria began a war for independence from France. Algeria won its independence in 1962, but the negotiations at the conclusions of the fighting involved an agreement that French companies would remain in control of the oil from the Sahara.

The British and American companies were also aware that they were heavily—perhaps too heavily—dependent on oil from the Persian Gulf and expanded their exploration efforts to Africa. A joint venture between Shell (an American company) and British Petroleum discovered oil in Nigeria's Niger River in 1956.

Several oil companies had also targeted the North African nation of Libya, especially after geological reports in the mid-1950s suggested that oil was likely to be found there. But Libya had learned from the experiences of the Persian Gulf nations and decided to negotiate a very different type of deal with the oil companies. "I did not want Libya to begin as Iraq or as Saudi Arabia or as Kuwait," said the Libyan petroleum minister in 1955. "I didn't want my country to be in the hands of one oil company."[13] First, Libya offered much smaller concession areas, rather than vast stretches of land. Second, Libya decided to award many of its concessions to smaller, independent companies that did not already have vast oil concessions in the region in the belief that they would have less of a conflict of interest that would prevent them from exploring and producing as much oil as could be found. In April 1959, Standard Oil of New Jersey made the first big discovery of oil in Libya, and by 1961, the country had begun exporting oil. By 1965, the country was the world's sixth-largest exporter of oil.

As these new sources began to pour their oil into the global market, prices fell even further. Gradually, the OPEC members began to understand the wisdom of prorationing—the need to alter their rate of production in response to upward and downward turns of the oil market, lowering production when necessary.

In November 1964, OPEC passed a resolution that reflected its concern about the continuing decline of crude oil prices. An Economic Commission was established to study price changes in the international oil market and come up with recommendations for appropriate responses to those price changes.

Libya became a member of OPEC in 1962 and hosted the Ninth OPEC Conference in Tripoli, Libya's capital, in July 1965. At this meeting, OPEC adopted its first production program, viewed at the time as a temporary response to the glut of oil on the world market. The plan was to allow only limited increases for each of the member nations: Venezuela and Indonesia were granted the right to increase production by 4 percent, Qatar by 6 percent, Saudi Arabia and Iraq by 9 percent, Iran by 16 percent, and Libya by 33 percent. However, the member nations had no intention of following these guidelines. Libya, in particular, whose oil production was in its newest stages and providing vast amounts of revenue to the country, declared that it would not only *not* accept the 33 percent limit, it would never accept any limits on its oil production.[14] Saudi Arabia and Iran were equally outspoken in their criticism of the production limits, and by June 1967, the effort to establish prorationing had quietly been put aside by OPEC.

In these early years, the aims of OPEC were often in conflict with the aims of its members; OPEC wanted to control production in the interest of a good financial return to all its members, while the member countries wanted to increase their own revenues from oil. The balance of power was, therefore, still firmly in the hands of the oil companies, who were actively seeking new sources of oil so they could keep providing more than enough oil for whoever needed it. As long as the oil market was a buyers' market, with plenty of cheap oil available to whoever wanted to buy it, OPEC would struggle.

As a result, OPEC spent its first years as a relatively weak and ineffective organization. OPEC had no real authority and no way to force its members to comply with decisions or policies. The OPEC members agreed to hold regular meetings to coordinate their policies, but they still were focused on establishing policies that best served their separate national interests. They wanted to find new customers for their oil; they wanted to develop their oil industries; they wanted to increase their share of the world market; they wanted to continue to explore and develop new oil fields in their countries.

A SELLERS' MARKET

While the conditions in the early 1960s had been a buyers' market—plenty of cheap oil for whoever wanted to buy it—the events in the late 1960s gradually changed the oil market into a sellers' market. Those years, from 1967 to 1971, would prove crucial to OPEC's survival as an organization and would see the rise of its influence.

Developments in world politics, specifically two events related to the Arab-Israeli War of 1967—the resulting eight-year closure of the Suez Canal and the use of oil as a bargaining chip—and civil war in Nigeria, marked the beginning of this change.

The first event was Egypt's closure of the Suez Canal. (The Suez Canal is an artificial, 100-mile-long canal in Egypt that connects the Red Sea with the Mediterranean Sea, providing a shortcut between oil fields in the Persian Gulf and the Middle East and oil consumers in western Europe.) With the canal closed, oil tankers were forced to carry their cargo south around Africa and then north to Europe. This lengthy journey not only added time but significantly increased the costs of transporting the oil.

But this was only one of the consequences of the Arab-Israeli War. The second event occurred when the Arab nations called for an oil embargo against countries who remained friendly to Israel, their enemy in the war. More specifically, Saudi Arabia, Kuwait, Iraq, Libya, and Algeria banned shipments of oil to the United States and Great Britain. Within two days, the flow of oil from the Arab nations had been reduced by 60 percent; the flow from Libya and Saudi Arabia was completely cut off.

When war broke out in the Middle East and Nigeria, the international oil market plunged into crisis as production came to a standstill. Egypt nationalized the Suez Canal *(above)* in 1956, but blocked the waterway by sinking several ships in it when an international coalition tried to take control of the area. Without the canal, oil distribution slowed drastically, exacerbating the oil crisis.

The third event was a civil war in Nigeria. New sources of oil had been uncovered in Nigeria's eastern region, and the people living there wanted a greater share of the oil revenue, a request the Nigerian government refused. As a result, the eastern region attempted to secede, declaring itself an independent nation known as Biafra. A brutal civil war followed, and the oil supply began to slow as the Nigerian government focused on fighting.

In spite of these events and the resulting pressures, the oil companies were able to continue supplying oil as needed.

The individual oil-producing nations suffered most, as loss of oil revenue crippled their economies. By March 1974, the oil embargo was lifted. The use of oil as a weapon had failed—for now.

THE LIBYAN MODEL

The cost of transporting oil rose steadily after the embargo, but demand for oil was also growing. It would take the actions of one OPEC member—Libya—to demonstrate how to use these two factors to dramatically strengthen the position of the oil-producing countries.

In September 1969, a military-led revolution against the monarchy (which had been closely allied with Western leaders) took place in Libya. Previously, Libya had been represented in oil negotiations by ministers who had little knowledge of the oil business, but this changed under the direction of Libya's new leader, Colonel Muammar Qaddafi.

Shortly after seizing power, Qaddafi contacted the 21 oil companies operating in Libya and announced that the new government would require new negotiations. Qaddafi's goal was to raise the price of crude oil in Libya, and publicly and privately, he took steps to make it clear to the oil companies that a new regime was in power. His public speeches declared that Libyan oil had been priced too low in relation to its production costs, its high quality, and its ease of transport to Western markets, especially western European markets.[15] In addition, it was announced that the oil companies must immediately begin drilling for oil in any concessions where drilling had not yet begun.

He also invited oil experts from Algeria, the Arab oil states, and the Soviets to visit Libya and form cooperative agreements that would help with the training of oil workers and engineers. Libya no longer wanted to rely on the expertise of foreign oil companies; it wanted to develop its own team of expert technicians to oversee the country's oil industry. Strategically, Libya then determined to negotiate not with the

(continues on page 36)

THE END OF SUBURBIA?

In 1946, the Levitt company purchased 4,000 acres of potato fields in Hempstead, New York, and started to build the largest housing development the country had seen at that time. The Levitts perfected the art of mass-producing houses and built several subdivisions in the northeast, including Levittowns in Bucks County, Pennsylvania, and Willingboro Township, New Jersey. Through low-interest government loan programs, World War II veterans and their families were able to purchase three- and four-bedroom homes in these new neighborhoods outside of the city for $11,500–$14,500. Although the communities had their own school systems, libraries, city halls, and grocery shops, drivers had to travel to the closest city center to work and for department store shopping.

Suburban sprawl, a term used to describe the spreading of a city and its suburbs over rural land, was built on the accessibility of cheap oil. The ability of citizens to own and operate cheap automobiles gave people a level of mobility that changed the way we live, work, and play, and how we get there and back. But is this too much of a good thing?

As more and more farmland becomes less available due to increased construction of new homes and superstores, as people become more environmentally aware of carbon emissions, and as fuel prices rise and the demand for oil outpaces Earth's ability to supply it, has this social experiment failed? Rather than "desuburbanization," some people think that a solution to this problem may be to reconfigure communities into walkable neighborhoods where needs are available within walking distance and to actively promote telecommuting (working from home), or equip neighborhood facilities with fax machines, copiers, and televideo equipment. Others promote steering drivers away from petroleum-fueled vehicles and toward cars that use alternative

An aerial view of a suburban development in Levittown, New York, 1950s.

energy. Richard Gilbert and Anthony Perl, the authors of *Transport Revolutions: Moving Freight and People Without Oil*, portray a future where oil production had hit its peak and started declining as early as 2012. According to Gilbert and Perl, Personal Rapid Transports (one- to six-person cars linked to overhead power grids that move along streets in designated guideways) will replace gas-guzzling vehicles and railways will be reconfigured to run on electricity. Air travel will be utilized exclusively by the rich. The authors say, "We've got to act now to avoid the conflict

(continues)

(continued)

and chaos that will ensue if oil demand doesn't drop in tandem with its declining availability and affordability."* In January 2008, Israel announced plans to develop an electric car network by 2011, but not enough countries have followed suit.

---

* Barbara Yaffe, "Life Without Transport by Oil Is Closer Than We Think," *The Vancouver Sun*, April 3, 2008. Available online at *http://www.canada.com/vancou versun/news/editorial/story.html?id=a5a37e1e-3d2c-4b11-8313-4125a1d4cd3f.*

(continued from page 33)

oil companies as a block, but with individual companies— playing the needs of one company against another, the same strategy the oil companies had used when negotiating with OPEC nations in the early 1960s. In another strategic move, Libya announced a plan to coordinate policies with Algeria, a fellow OPEC member that was taking steps to increase the price of its crude oil.

Finally, Libya began cutting back the production of several oil companies, particularly the smaller, independent companies, in order to decrease the amount of oil available to European markets. Ultimately, the oil companies were forced to agree to Libya's demand for an increase in oil prices. Libya's actions would become a model for other OPEC nations.

All of this was possible because what had once been a buyers' market was clearly transforming into a sellers' market. From 1949 to 1972, world energy consumption more than tripled, and demand for oil grew more than five and a half times. By 1969, the market was quite different and Libya's negotiating position was far stronger than before. By that time, consumption in western Europe had grown 15 times, and Libya was supplying more than 25 percent of western Europe's oil.[16] This was a dramatic development in a region that had traditionally relied upon its own carbon-based energy resource (coal); certain regions were rich in coal, and coal-mining had been an important livelihood for many who lived in those areas. Suddenly, cheap imported oil began to compete with, and ultimately overtake, coal, forcing the closing of many coal mines.

Outside Europe, industrial growth and improved standards of living in the two decades after World War II had contributed to surges in oil consumption. In Japan, consumption of oil grew 137 times over; in the United States, consumption tripled as city populations migrated to the suburbs, more products were transported from place to place and across the country by truck, train, tanker, and plane, and cars became a new standard of prosperity.[17] (From 1949 to 1972, the number of cars—increasingly longer and wider cars—in the United States grew from 45 million to 119 million.[18] Gas mileage was not an issue.) As cars became more common, people no longer had to live in cities or within access to buses, trains, or subways. New housing developments sprang up farther and farther from cities, followed by shopping malls, drive-in restaurants, and construction of new highways.

To fuel this increasing number of cars, more gas stations sprang up, dotting American roads, all seeking to build loyalty for their brand of gasoline by offering American consumers "extras." For some, it was special service—uniformed attendants would check tires and oil and wash windows while they filled drivers' tanks with gas. For other stations, it was products—collectible drinking glasses or records of children's music or special toy trucks with the gas company logo on them. It was a way of life fueled by oil, and dependent on foreign sources to provide that fuel. Provided that the oil continued to flow, affluent Americans could continue their suburban migration. But the nation's prosperity was actually in the hands of oil-producing nations.

From
Abundance
to Crisis

WHEN WE THINK OF OIL-PRODUCING NATIONS, WE GENERALLY think of the nations that make up OPEC, or perhaps more often we simply think of a select group of nations in the Middle East. But the story of an American economy built on oil began in a small town in Pennsylvania, and it is important to understand those beginnings to appreciate the events that led to the energy crisis of the 1970s and the rise of OPEC.

Those who lived in the mid-nineteenth century were familiar with the idea of energy as a precious resource. The lamps that brightened their homes were lit using whale oil, but the numbers of sperm whales were dwindling, nearly to the point of extinction, and the hunt was on for some new source of fuel that would power their lights. In Europe, a new process had been pioneered for digging oil out of the ground by hand, refining it, and using it as a new source of power. That new fuel was kerosene.

About the same time, a group of investors based in New Haven, Connecticut, had learned that the same type of substance existed in the hills of Pennsylvania. They formed the Pennsylvania Rock Oil Company in 1857 to extract this "rock oil." Soon, the Pennsylvania Rock Oil Company had decided to try a new technique for extraction. Rather than digging the oil out of the rocks by hand, they would use a drilling technique similar to that used for salt wells. A man named Edwin Drake was chosen to lead the enterprise. Drake and his team headed for the small town of Titusville, Pennsylvania, and set up their base at a farm where oil was seeping out of the ground in a kind of spring. They dug for six months without success. Finally, Drake had spent all of the money the investors had provided for the effort, and they sent him a letter telling him to give up. But, just before the letter reached him, Drake tried one final well. That final well yielded the oil that would change everything. He collected the first oil in 42-gallon whiskey barrels; the measurement became the standard used by the oil industry. The price of that barrel of oil in January 1861: $10.

After the Civil War (1861–1865), thousands of prospectors, many of them veterans, headed to Titusville, intent on finding oil and becoming wealthy. Towns like Oil City and Pithole soon sprang up around Titusville. As more and more oil was drilled, a glut of oil caused the price of a barrel to drop, mirroring the laws of supply and demand that still shape the industry today. Prices reached a low of 10¢ a barrel barely a year after those first barrels were selling for $10 each. As a result, those early oil towns were abandoned.

This early experience in the oil industry—the tale of what happened in the oil fields of Pennsylvania—is a powerful example of what has happened, on progressively larger scales, when

In 1900, California produced 4 million barrels of oil and by 1910 production had jumped to 77 million barrels. Oil prospectors saw a decrease in production in the late 1910s until the discovery of three major oil fields: Huntington Beach, Santa Fe Springs, and Signal Hill (above). Nearby towns were filled with activity as people built roads, houses, and oil derricks as part of the growing oil industry.

oil was discovered in other parts of the world. In reality, it is not that the oil wells run dry—in fact, some 4,000 small oil wells are still active across Pennsylvania.[19] But as oil fields get older, or "mature," in the language of the oil industry, the easy-to-access oil near the surface has already been extracted; what remains is more difficult to extract and therefore more costly to produce. Frequently these more mature fields are simply abandoned in favor of cheaper, newer fields in other locations, and those who have built their livelihoods on the oil business are left with an economy in shambles.

Because the Middle East has such a rich supply of oil and because that oil is so inexpensive to produce, it has become the dominant player in the oil market. And increasingly, it is OPEC that determines supply and sets prices. Americans had, perhaps, been unaware of how dependent they had become on OPEC nations to supply their energy needs. That ignorance quickly came to an end in the 1970s, when an oil embargo from Arab nations and a series of OPEC price increases made it clear that the OPEC nations and not the Western oil companies were in control at the pump.

PARTICIPATION

In the early 1970s, the control that Western-based oil companies had long enjoyed over the world's oil fields began to fade. From the beginning, Western oil companies had operated in foreign countries through a system of "concessions," contracts with rulers that gave oil companies the right to own, explore, and market oil in a specific territory. In some cases these concessionary territories were quite large, such as the 480,000 square miles in what was then Persia (now Iran) that had been granted to a British explorer; in other cases—Libya, for example—the idea of much smaller concessions, such as the 2,000 square miles granted to the Occidental Petroleum Corporation, was being pioneered.[20]

But increasingly, particularly as their expertise in the oil industry grew, the countries wanted their own people to run their own part of the oil industry. They were no longer interested in giving away control to foreigners. The oil was theirs. In the same way that OPEC had provided a forum for greater control over pricing, the oil-producing nations now wanted greater control over production.

Some countries resorted to outright nationalization—simply seizing the oil fields and declaring that they were no longer private property, but property of the state, or the nation. This was successfully done in Russia in 1917 and was attempted in Iran in 1951. The threat of nationalization pressured the oil companies into negotiating, or at least it increased the willingness of the oil companies to negotiate. The term that OPEC members used was "participation." Participation provided the oil-producing countries a greater say in their own natural resource, without forcing them into the market to compete with the international oil companies in marketing or distribution. OPEC threatened cutbacks if companies did not agree, and swiftly, to greater participation.

Saudi Arabian oil minister Zaki Yamani, who had attended both New York University and Harvard Law School, was placed in charge of negotiating as the representative of OPEC. "There is a worldwide trend toward nationalization and Saudis cannot stand against it alone," Yamani stated. "The industry should realize this and come to terms so that they can save as much as possible under the circumstances."[21]

The oil companies reluctantly agreed, but Algeria, Libya, and Kuwait refused to sign any agreement. Libya proceeded to nationalize several of the oil operations there, its leader, Qaddafi, proudly stating that he had given the United States "a big hard blow" on "its cold insolent face."[22] Other blows would follow.

OIL AS A WEAPON

It was another conflict between a group of Arab nations and Israel that would once again lead to the use of oil as a weapon, this time with devastating consequences for the United States. In the late spring and early summer of 1973, Egyptian leader Anwar Sadat made clear his view that the land captured by Israel in the 1967 war—the Sinai and Golan Heights—still rightfully belonged to the Arab nations. In addition, Israeli settlers had moved into Hebron, a town on the West Bank of the Jordan River. Hebron had been seized in the war, but as part of the cease-fire agreement, settlement had been forbidden. Sadat began meeting with other Arab leaders, making secret plans for a joint military effort against Israel.

Behind the scenes, the perception was that the United States was a supporter of Israel, while the Soviet Union was a

In October 1973, Egypt and Syria declared war on Israel to regain territories lost after the Six-Day War of 1967. Although Israel retained control of the territories, the war marked the first time the oil-producing Arab countries successfully used oil as a political weapon against Western nations. Pictured are the ruins of Quneitra, the former capital of the Golan Heights, a region formerly located in southwestern Syria.

supporter of the Arab nations—a perception based in part on military aid and technical assistance, as well as general financial assistance, provided by the two nations to their allies.

At least one leader—King Faisal of Saudi Arabia—warned the oil companies operating in his country that oil might be used as a weapon in the brewing conflict if the United States did not take swift steps to withdraw its support for Israeli policies. Through Oil Minister Yamani, he cautioned the oil companies that the king was "one hundred percent determined to effect a change in U.S. policy and to use oil for that purpose."[23] The oil companies relayed the warning, but intelligence services in the region took a different view—they suggested that Israel had clear military superiority and that an Arab attack would be suicidal. The intelligence sources were confident that war would not occur.

A meeting was scheduled for October 8, 1973, between representatives of OPEC and representatives of the oil companies. The meeting had been called by OPEC because the oil-producing nations wanted a new deal. Market prices for oil were going up, and the OPEC nations wanted a greater share of those profits. But, as representatives traveled to the meeting, they learned that the intelligence estimates had been incorrect. On October 6, Israel was attacked from the south by Egypt, whose troops crossed the Suez Canal, and from the north by Syria, which quickly occupied Golan Heights.

The conflict had a clear and immediate effect on the negotiating teams. The American oil officials knew they had been warned oil might be used as a weapon, and fighting had now begun. The OPEC nations, at least the Arab delegates, were excited by the news of early Arab victories and felt that they were, at last, negotiating from a clear position of strength. They wanted a 100 percent increase in the price of their oil, or an additional three dollars per barrel. The oil companies were offering something considerably smaller: a 15 percent increase, or an additional 45 cents per barrel.

An increase the size of what the OPEC nations were demanding would have a dramatic impact on the economies of the oil-consuming nations, particularly on consumers, who would certainly feel the effects of such a large price increase. From October 9 to 11, the oil company representatives frantically contacted governments in Western Europe, Japan, and the United States, but the response was clear: The price increase requested was too large and could not be agreed to.

The fighting was in its sixth day when the representatives of the oil companies notified Yamani, who was acting as the chief OPEC negotiator, that they could not make a counteroffer that would be acceptable. Yamani placed a phone call, spoke quickly in Arabic, and then informed the oil company representatives, "They're mad at you."[24] The negotiations were at an end.

ENERGY CRISIS

A more informal gathering took place the following day. In this meeting, the delegates discussed how oil might be used as part of the still-ongoing Arab-Israeli conflict. The representative from Iraq was quick to argue that it was the United States that was supplying Israel with weapons to use against the Arab nations, and so the United States should suffer the consequences of its actions. All American businesses in the Arab world should immediately be nationalized, he argued; all Arab money should immediately be withdrawn from American banks; and no oil should be supplied to the United States or any other nation friendly to Israel. Several of the ministers, including the Algerian chairman and Yamani, argued that this was not in the best interests of the OPEC nations. The Iraq delegation then left the meeting.

The idea of a total embargo had been dismissed as impractical, but a more structured embargo soon found favor with the remaining delegates. By the end of the meeting, the Arab oil ministers had agreed to cut production by five percent from the previous month's levels, and then to keep cutting it by five percent each month until their objectives were met. Only so-called "friendly states" would continue to receive oil at the previous levels. The United States was to be subjected to the most severe cuts.[25]

On October 16, OPEC delegates from the Persian Gulf nations met in Kuwait City. They announced their decision to raise the price of oil by 70 percent, to $5.11 a barrel.

This was a historic turning point that reshaped OPEC's role in the global economy. No longer would the oil companies be setting the price of oil, nor would there be negotiations to determine what that price would be. Control over the price of oil was now firmly in the hands of the oil producers, and the levels of production were now a matter of international politics, not industry practice. Oil could be used as a reward and a punishment.

The effects of the failed OPEC negotiations were not immediately felt; instead, the focus in the United States and much of the international community was on bringing the war in the Middle East to a quick end. Gradually, with the help of outside supplies and a stream of reserve soldiers (the Soviet Union provided Syria and Egypt with supplies; the United States did the same for Israel), the Israeli forces were able to push Syria's troops back from the Golan Heights and, similarly, force the Egyptian troops away from the Suez Canal.

A cease-fire was approved on October 22—the fighting had officially lasted only 16 days, but its repercussions would be significant.

SHOCK AND RESPONSE

The combination of the partial and progressive oil embargo and OPEC's price hike quickly caused panic as countries assessed their supplies and scrambled to find new sources. From the $5.11-per-barrel price OPEC had announced in October, the price rose to $16 per barrel in less than a month. Suddenly, new attention was paid to oil in Alaska, in the North Sea between England and Norway, and on the continent of Africa. These sources had not been tapped as much because the oil was more expensive to extract, but production was nonetheless quickly increased as a response to the embargo.

At the same time, new technologies were explored—seismic surveys and advanced drilling techniques, geochemistry, and improvements in geology—to show where new oil deposits might be tapped and quickly exploited. However, many of these solutions would only bear fruit in the longer term.

In the United States, the administration of then-President Richard Nixon quietly drafted plans to send troops to seize oil fields in Saudi Arabia, Kuwait, and Oman, plans that were ultimately scrapped.[26] Instead, the government took steps to ration

OPEC was able to institute an oil embargo against nations sympathetic to Israel during the Arab-Israeli conflict, an event that triggered a worldwide gas crisis. Production and supply to countries like the United States were drastically reduced, leaving many citizens desperate for gas as it became expensive and scarce (above).

oil throughout the country. Soon, Americans were waiting in line to buy gas. Some stations made gas available at certain times based upon whether customers' license plates ended with an odd or even number; others only sold gas on certain days of the week; still others sold as usual as long as their supply lasted. Drivers were often forced to wait in lines, some for an hour or more, to buy gas. They stopped driving altogether, if they could, and others bought smaller cars. In a symbolic sign of the energy shortage, the White House did not light its Christmas tree that year.

When Western European nations publicly announced their support for the Arab position in the disputed Golan Heights and Gaza territories, the OPEC embargo against them was lifted; it was not until the spring of 1974 that oil shipments were finally resumed to the United States. OPEC had demonstrated beyond a doubt that it could control not only the price of oil but also, to a great extent, its availability throughout the world.

The United States swiftly took steps to protect itself against future efforts by OPEC nations to use oil to influence global politics. In 1975, Congress passed the Energy Policy and Conservation Act, establishing—for the first time—fuel economy standards for American cars and trucks. That same year, under President Gerald Ford, Congress created the Strategic Petroleum Reserve (SPR), which would provide an

 POSITIVE OUTCOMES FROM THE OIL EMBARGO

The 1973 oil embargo had dramatic results around the world, not all of them negative. In the United States, Congress issued a national maximum speed limit of 55 miles per hour on highways, which decreased the number of automobile fatalities. Automobile makers reduced the size of their cars, and many drivers turned to smaller, more compact cars that used front-wheel drive and consumed less fuel. Gasoline stations closed on Sundays and families turned the thermostats in their homes down to 65 degrees. The energy crisis also led to greater interest in researching alternative power, such as wind and solar power, and the government approved the Trans-Alaska Pipeline, in order to capitalize on domestic oil.

Japan managed well compared to other oil-importing countries. Japanese automakers became the worldwide leaders in energy-efficient, compact models, a position they still hold today. Japan's economy also shifted from oil-intensive industries to electronics and similar businesses.

emergency supply of crude oil that could be accessed during a future crisis. The SPR was designed with the plan of storing a billion barrels of oil—at the time, enough to provide 90 days of oil to keep America running—in empty salt mines in Louisiana and Texas. It was a kind of massive insurance policy against future oil embargoes—an insurance policy that, over the next 20 years, the United States would spend some $37 billion to create, fill, and maintain.[27]

The SPR has never been fully tested or utilized. However, it continues to be accessed by presidents in times of energy uncertainty, proof that the actions taken by OPEC in 1973 continue to resonate in current energy policies.

The Soviet Union, which was a net oil exporter, did better than before the oil crisis. The increase in foreign currency reserves allowed for the import of grains and other foodstuffs, kept military spending down, and increased production of consumer goods.

Oil imports were cut in Brazil by about $50 billion with the development of Proálcool, a program sponsored by the government to phase out the use of fossil fuels in favor of ethanol. Ethanol fuel, which in Brazil is made from cheap sugar cane, is mixed with gasoline to produce gasohol (24% alcohol blended with 76% gasoline). The program successfully reduced by 10 million the number of cars that use only gasoline in Brazil, thereby reducing the country's dependence on oil imports. Although domestic oil consumption still outweighs ethanol consumption, today Brazil is the second-largest producer of ethanol, is considered to have the world's first sustainable biofuels economy, and is the biofuel industry leader.

The SPR was finally ready in 1984 but, since its creation, has seldom been used, and in those few cases when it was tapped, its use was triggered by a factor other than an OPEC embargo or other OPEC-related cause. In 1990, as the United States prepared for the first Gulf War, 17 million barrels were released from the SPR, an act that led to a fall in price, from $27 a barrel to $21. In 2000, President Bill Clinton released oil from the SPR in response to a heating oil shortage. And, after Hurricane Katrina devastated the Gulf Coast in August 2005, the Energy Department lent 12 million barrels of crude oil to refiners under an agreement that required the 12 million barrels be returned, with interest, when the effects of the storm had passed.[28]

The decision of whether to tap into the SPR remains in the hands of the American president, and is no simple process. If the president decides that a particular crisis, or "supply interruption" (in the language used by SPR staff), makes it necessary to release oil from the reserve, approximately one month of oil could be pumped out at full speed before the volume would begin to drop off. Because the SPR has never been tested in a large-scale emergency, no one can be completely sure how effective it would be. The oil would need to be mixed once extracted before being shipped to refineries.[29] Perhaps most significantly, all of the SPR sites are capable of pumping out only 4.4 million barrels a day when operating at full capacity—about a third of what the United States imports daily.[30]

In January 2007, President George W. Bush announced a plan to expand SPR facilities to hold 1.5 billion barrels, enough— according to then-Energy Secretary Samuel W. Bodman—for an "approximately 97 day supply of net import protection."[31] The expansion would not happen immediately, but instead be a gradual process of purchasing crude oil at a steady rate. The project was targeted for completion by 2027.

4

OPEC's Golden Age

THE OPEC OIL EMBARGO PROVIDED AN INCENTIVE FOR WEST-
ern nations to begin reconsidering their view that oil was plentiful and cheap. The embargo demonstrated that oil had become
a key element to the global economy and proved that the oil
ministers from a handful of nations were suddenly among the
world's most influential men. For four years, from 1974 to 1978,
OPEC's headquarters in Vienna, Austria, was the site of important international diplomacy. A former secretary-general of
OPEC later described this period as "OPEC's Golden Age."[32]

The Golden Age began with an OPEC meeting in Tehran,
Iran, in late December 1973. The meeting was being held to
determine the official price of oil, but that decision had other
considerations. First, certain members were concerned that too

high a price increase might trigger a global depression. Second, some, particularly the Saudis, wanted to reemphasize that the embargo was a political move, intended to correct an imbalance of global power as much as it was meant to reclaim control of resources in their territories.

The decision was to increase the price to $11.65 per barrel, an act that the shah of Iran energetically argued for. (This price increase was significant: in 1970, oil had been priced at $1.80 per barrel; in 1971, the price was raised to $2.18; in mid-1973, the price was again raised, to $2.90; and in October 1973, to $5.12.) The price had quadrupled since the Arab-Israeli War.

The price increase created a tremendous financial gain for oil-exporting countries: $7 on each barrel sold.[33] In five years, from 1972 to 1977, the combined petroleum earnings of oil exporters had risen from $23 billion to $140 billion.[34] The nations were faced with an interesting dilemma: how to spend the incredible amounts of cash they were now receiving.

The oil-exporting countries were, for the most part, governed by a single leader or a royal family who had little interest in ensuring that the oil wealth would make its way down to ordinary citizens. Rarely was money spent on improving healthcare or creating new jobs for the poorer citizens. Instead, money was spent on building elaborate palaces, on acquiring new symbols of wealth, on weapons and arms, and, of course, on cars. Because fuel was so cheap and plentiful, cars began to dot the landscape throughout the Middle East.

For four years, the spending continued—until what had been a huge financial surplus turned into a deficit. Incredibly, the OPEC nations spent away all the wealth they had obtained from the price hikes. In 1974, OPEC had a $67 billion surplus; by 1978, the surplus had turned into a $2 billion deficit.[35] OPEC's Golden Age was done!

The Western world tended to view OPEC as a single entity, as an organization acting in unison. That image was symbolized,

From 1974–1978, OPEC members brought in vast revenues from increasing oil prices. Leaders of oil-exporting countries benefited financially by accessing their countries' natural resources, but rarely did the money make its way down to the people. Pictured is a bedroom in the Sadabad Palace, the summer complex of the Pahlavi dynasty (1925–1979) in Tehran, Iran. Today the complex is a museum.

in the 1970s, by Ahmed Yamani, the Saudi oil minister whose every vague comment was used by journalists intent on determining what would happen to oil—and the global economy—in the future.[36]

In reality, however, Yamani's prominence, and the assumption that he actually spoke for OPEC as a whole, sparked intense criticism from other OPEC oil ministers. To them, his visibility in the Western media suggested he was disloyal to his king and to all Arabs.

Another thorn in the side of a unified OPEC was the courting of the shah of Iran by a stream of American presidents. His lobbying efforts sparked dismay in Saudi Arabia, particularly, which feared an Iran that was too prominent in the Middle East.

So, while OPEC seemed to present a united front in setting the price of oil, the divisions between countries within OPEC were many. Those differences emerged even more during the so-called Golden Age and became more prominent as the years of surplus came to an end.

REVOLUTION

The story of Iran offers a useful lesson about the dangers of an economy based on vast revenues from oil. The fortune that swept into Iran during the mid-1970s was spent—or misspent—on symbols of modernization, things like vast highways and gleaming new buildings in Tehran (Iran's capital). While these acts were part of the shah's effort to bring his country into the twentieth century, little thought was given to the impact that a dramatic change in the economy would have on the average Iranian.

As tales of new wealth and new opportunity spread throughout Iran, villagers left their homes and hurried into cities, which quickly became overcrowded and provided no job opportunities for the uneducated, untrained young men who came. In addition, as small family farms were abandoned, Iran's agricultural output declined, and food and other products had to be imported from other countries. Prices began to increase. The cost of living increased.

Meanwhile, all around were symbols of wealth, and the shah did little to curb his own lavish lifestyle, ignoring the growing discontent of his people. The deep divisions between the "haves" and "have-nots" finally erupted in protests against the shah and the perceived Western influence on his reign. Revolution followed, and in December 1978, oil exports from

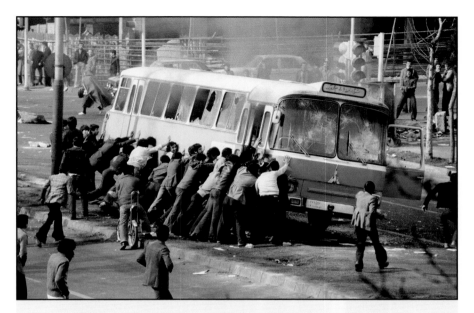

The Shah Pahlavi's close ties with the West, his lavish lifestyle, and his efforts to modernize the country brought about strikes and demonstrations throughout the country. Eventually, the shah was deposed in October 1979 and sent into exile. When oil production in Iran stopped, other OPEC members provided extra oil to make up the difference.

Iran ceased. To help counterbalance this disruption, several other OPEC nations (including Saudi Arabia) quickly boosted their output. But Iran had been the second-largest exporter in the world, and Western policymakers feared that the drop in production would lead to a crippling shortage.

What followed was a panic, based in part on the experiences of 1973. Governments began buying up vast quantities of oil, well beyond what was actually needed, in order to stockpile supplies in case the price began to rise dramatically. This effect went right down the consumption chain from the oil companies to the governments to even the average American consumer who, fearing price increases, did not allow his or her gas tank to go less than three-quarters full. All of this created an additional 3 million barrels per day of demand beyond what was actually being consumed.[37]

In March 1979, OPEC met again and determined that its members could add whatever additional surcharges they wanted to their official prices, meaning that oil could be sold for whatever someone was willing to pay. The Saudis stood alone in opposition to this "free-for-all," fearing that a dramatic increase in prices would spur Western nations to find alternate sources of energy or take other action. The Saudis suggested that whatever short-term gains the exporters might enjoy from a sudden price spike would end in a much more catastrophic loss of revenue in the long term. The Saudis officially announced that they would maintain the official prices, without adding any surcharges. It is important to note, however, that they did cut production in mid-1979, which helped to increase prices anyway.

By the late 1970s, the price of oil had risen to $34 a barrel. But in the early 1980s, the energy market began to change again, as efforts in Alaska, the North Sea, and Mexico began to bear fruit. Besides these new sources of oil, new sources of energy—coal (in a comeback), nuclear power, and natural gas—and efforts to promote conservation and energy efficiency also began to pay off. Demand for oil was falling, and OPEC would need to adjust.

CUTTING PRODUCTION

In 1977, two-thirds of the total crude oil in the West had come from OPEC; by 1982, non-OPEC production had overtaken that of OPEC, and was on the rise.[38] As a result, OPEC oil ministers found themselves needing to make a difficult choice—either cut prices to recapture the market that was going to non-OPEC sources, or cut production to maintain the price of oil. They did not want to cut prices so, in March

1982, they voted to cut production to a total output of 18 million barrels per day (the output had been 31 million barrels per day in 1979). To meet that limit, each country—except Saudi Arabia—had its own individual quota, based on population and oil reserves; Saudi Arabia was charged with adjusting its output, as a "swing producer," to adjust the overall total. (In that role, all of the other OPEC nations would fulfill their quotas first, and the difference between what they produced and what was demanded became Saudi Arabia's share, to be produced by Saudi Arabia. For example, if the production of the OPEC members totaled 12.5 million barrels per day and OPEC had established an overall quota ceiling of 18 million barrels per day; the difference between the 12.5 million and the 18 million was left to be produced by Saudi Arabia.) These quotas were meant to be temporary, a response to an uncertain market. However, they would linger far longer.

Competition, particularly from British North Sea oil, contributed greatly to OPEC's decision to cut production; before long, that competition grew, causing prices to tumble and, for the first time, forcing OPEC to cut its prices—in March 1983, the fixed price was lowered from $34 a barrel to $29. A year later, the price was decreased again, to $28. Soon, the prices would begin to fall more dramatically.

OPEC's deputy secretary general from 1978 to 1989, Fadhil J. Al-Chalabi, later noted:

> OPEC's pricing policies of the 1970s and early 1980s, which enabled its average price to reach the staggering level of $36 per barrel . . . were self-defeating for its members, especially for those with enormous proven reserves and increasing export capacities. Very high prices brought OPEC oil under an increasing pressure, leading to a continual fall in the organization's share in the world market.[39]

OPEC's use of meeting to establish fixed prices made it practically impossible for its members to compete with non-OPEC producers, who were free to raise and lower prices based on supply and demand. As a result, buyers went first to non-OPEC sources, whose prices were generally lower. OPEC oil became the "back-up" supply, a resource tapped when other supplies were exhausted.

For the oil-producing nations, this was a disastrous development. Oil was their principal source of revenue, and a sudden drop in that income had a severe impact on their economies. In order to maintain a set price, production was cut again and again. Unfortunately, that meant that Saudi Arabia, in its role as "swing producer," took a continual decline in production as the continuing decrease in world demand for OPEC oil meant production was lowered.[40] It was a role that Saudi Arabia could not maintain indefinitely. As less and less Saudi oil was in demand, its influence within OPEC and on the world stage began to slip.

Finally, the Saudis had had enough. By late 1985, they began to alert OPEC and non-OPEC members that they could not continue to accept a declining share of the oil market. Meeting at the end of the year, OPEC (including Saudi Arabia) announced that the era of fixed pricing had come to an end; OPEC intended to aggressively battle with non-OPEC oil producers "to secure and defend a fair share in the world oil market consistent with the necessary income for member countries' development."[41]

The result of this change in policy was dramatic, and it caused the price of oil to collapse as OPEC members ignored not only the price restrictions but also their established production quotas. Instead, hundreds, even thousands, of business deals, day after day, determined how much oil would be sold and for what price.

This "oil collapse" affected not only OPEC members, but weighed heavily on non-OPEC members as well. In most cases, non-OPEC oil was more expensive to produce, and as cheap OPEC oil began to flood the market, it became harder and harder for non-OPEC sources to compete, let alone make their oil profitable.

Within OPEC, the sudden change in policy benefited some members more than others. Those with large oil reserves, like Saudi Arabia, Kuwait, Iraq, Nigeria, and Venezuela, were able to dramatically increase the output of their fields and so make enough of a profit to balance out the falling prices. But countries like Algeria, Ecuador, Gabon, Indonesia, Libya, and Qatar could not follow suit; they lacked the production capacity and marketing ability to make up for dropping prices. One result was an increase in tension within OPEC, with some members deeply dissatisfied at the change in pricing and production policies.

In December 1986, representatives of the OPEC countries gathered in Geneva, Switzerland, and negotiated a new agreement that included a new fixed price of around $18 per barrel and a loose quota system that would support that fixed price. Both OPEC and non-OPEC producers welcomed the new price, but it was an agreement that would be, at best, a temporary measure, as OPEC members quickly violated the approved quotas and pricing structures. Prices fell again.

In November 1988, OPEC formally dropped the fixed-price system. OPEC members were no longer forced to sell oil at a particular price, but quotas were still in place and loosely enforced. Finally, oil pricing was based on the market—on supply and demand.

War and Oil

ON AUGUST 2, 1990, IRAQI TROOPS INVADED KUWAIT, THE first volley in Iraqi leader Saddam Hussein's plan to seize the oil-rich country and make it part of Iraq. Iraq was still dealing with the financial impact of the devastating eight-year Iran-Iraq War (1980–1988) and hoped to seize Kuwait to create the largest oil power in the world. Indeed, if Hussein succeeded, he would have controlled 20 percent of OPEC's production and 25 percent of the world's oil reserves. With that much oil—and the wealth from it—under his control, he would have been in a position to dominate not only OPEC but also the global oil market. As U.S. president George H.W. Bush noted, "Our jobs, our way of life, our own freedom and the freedom of friendly countries around the world would all suffer if control of the world's great oil reserves fell into the hands of Saddam Hussein."[42]

When Saddam Hussein's Iraqi forces invaded Kuwait in 1990 (above), oil-dependent countries became concerned about the balance of power in OPEC. If Hussein conquered Kuwait, he would control a large percentage of the world's oil supply, allowing him to influence the international oil market. An international coalition was quickly formed to stop Hussein and protect and defend Kuwait.

With other world leaders fearing that Iraq would launch an invasion of Saudi Arabia once Kuwait had been successfully seized, the international community assembled an international coalition of troops, led by U.S. forces under Bush, to defend Kuwait.

This Persian Gulf War (1990–1991) created a crisis for OPEC because the act of one member attacking another (again) threatened the price of oil and, more importantly, the rights of its members to exist as independent states. The other OPEC members quickly supported the nations that made up the coalition that came to Kuwait's defense by increasing their oil production to compensate for oil lost from Iraq and Kuwait. Despite this action, oil prices began to rise as uncertainty about the supply—and other events in the Middle East—inspired many oil-consuming countries to stockpile oil in anticipation of future price hikes or supply interruptions.

Hussein's attempt to dominate the oil market and spread his anti-Western politics failed when the international coalition of troops was able to force Iraqi troops out of Kuwait. To seal the defeat, the United Nations announced an embargo against Iraqi oil (and Kuwaiti oil while it was under Iraqi control).

During this war, Saudi Arabia granted permission for the United States to station troops on its soil. The troops would not only serve as a launching point in the effort to force Iraqi troops out of Kuwait but would also protect the kingdom from Iraqi attack. Some of those American troops remained in the kingdom long after the war ended, a presence that sparked the anger of a former Saudi citizen, Osama bin Laden. Bin Laden would use the fact of foreign troops being on Saudi soil as a rallying cry to launch attacks against U.S. targets, first in the Middle East and later in New York and Washington, D.C., on September 11, 2001.

OIL FOR FOOD

Shortly after the Persian Gulf War ended, a mission from the United Nations traveled to Iraq to investigate claims of a humanitarian crisis. Indeed, the aftermath of years of war and the results of the oil embargo had caused suffering among the Iraqi population, and the United Nations spearheaded efforts to amend the embargo and allow the Iraqi government to sell limited amounts of oil in order to meet the basic needs of the Iraqi people.

Initially, Hussein refused the humanitarian offers, but, finally, in 1996, his government and the United Nations

The decades of war in Iraq and a UN embargo have devastated the country's economy. The Oil for Food Program, overseen by the UN from 1995–2003, allowed the Iraqi government to trade their oil for food, medicine, and other humanitarian aid. *Above*, an Iraqi woman collects her monthly allowance of sugar at a rationing station in January 1999.

reached agreement over an "oil for food" program, in which limited amounts of Iraqi oil could be sold to purchase basic needs, specifically food and medicine for the people. In the initial stages of the program, Iraq would be permitted to sell $2 billion worth of oil every six months, with two-thirds of that amount designated for use in meeting the nation's humanitarian needs. In 1998, the limit was raised to $5.26 billion every six months, again with two-thirds of the oil proceeds designated for humanitarian needs. The next year, in December 1999, the embargo limit on Iraqi oil exports was removed by the UN Security Council. (Some sources, including the U.S. General Accounting Office, now the Government Accountability Office, later suggested that Hussein took advantage of poor oversight in the program to accumulate more wealth.)

A CHANGING MARKET

After the Persian Gulf War, the market price of oil rose and fell depending more upon international economic and political events than other factors. When Asian economic growth and development created greater demand for oil, the price began to rise. As Russia poured oil into the market, prices experienced a downward pressure. Eventually, in order to keep the price of oil in the $20-per-barrel range, Russia and Mexico (two

 WORLD OIL PRODUCTION

Of the 14 countries exporting more than 1 million barrels of oil per day in 2004, 10 were OPEC members. (The world's largest non-OPEC oil exporters are Russia, Norway, Mexico, and Kazakhstan. The United States is currently the world's largest oil importer.)

Middle East:	29%
North America:	19%
Eastern Europe:	14%
Africa:	12%
Asia and Oceania:	10%
Western Europe:	8%
Central & South America:	8%

Source: EIA

non-OPEC nations) joined Saudi Arabia and Venezuela in an agreement to cut production.

The last years of the twentieth century were a challenging period for OPEC members. "In 1998 alone, OPEC members lost something in the region of $60 billion," said OPEC Secretary General Ali Rodríguez Araque. "That came as a cold, hard shock to our governments, who were forced to cut budgets and slash development spending. But it also acted as a sharp reminder as to how complacency can be one step away from a fall. That crisis pushed us to the very limits of the pain barrier."[43]

In 2001, when members of the terrorist group al-Qaeda attacked the United States on September 11, Saudi Arabia stepped in to lower the price of oil by tapping into its own reserve as a show of solidarity with the United States. When U.S. forces invaded Iraq in 2003, however, Saudi Arabia and other OPEC members allowed oil prices to rise, an economic sign of disapproval over the invasion of an OPEC member.

Oil has been an ongoing source of conflict in Iraq. Critics of the administration of President George W. Bush suggested that one of the principal goals in invading Iraq was not to eliminate Iraq's ability to use nuclear and biological weapons against the West (one of the stated goals of the invasion), but instead to secure Iraq's oil. Control of Iraq's oil fields poses continued threats to Iraq's stability. The majority of Iraq's oil fields are located in the northern region, traditionally populated by Iraq's Kurdish population. The presence of Iraq's oil resource in Kurdish land makes it unlikely that Kurds will be given an independent territory, one of their stated goals.

OPEC Today

IN THE 1970S, OPEC SUPPLIED ABOUT 67 PERCENT OF THE world's oil. Today, it supplies closer to 40 percent.[44] Because of uncertainty in the Persian Gulf, much of the world has turned to non-OPEC sources for oil. But some analysts suggest that those sources have already reached their peak capacity. According to oil analyst Charley Maxwell, production from major non-OPEC oil exporters began to peak and fall off in 1998: the United States recorded its highest production in 1970, Egypt in 1996, Argentina in 1998, Colombia in 1999, the United Kingdom's North Sea in 1999, Australia in 2000, Norway's North Sea in 2001, Oman in 2001, and Yemen in 2002, with Mexico and China nearing their peaks currently.[45] This will mean a steady shift in power back toward the OPEC nations, which still hold three-fourths of the world's proven oil reserves.

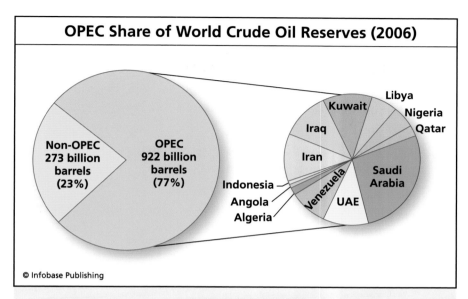

OPEC Share of World Crude Oil Reserves (2006)

Non-OPEC 273 billion barrels (23%)

OPEC 922 billion barrels (77%)

Indonesia
Angola
Algeria

Iran

Iraq

Kuwait

Libya

Nigeria

Qatar

Saudi Arabia

Venezuela

UAE

© Infobase Publishing

OPEC nations hold more than three-fourths of the world's oil reserves. Aging oil fields and a dearth of new ones has made it difficult for Indonesia to meet its quota. Indonesia, a member of OPEC since 1962, will quit the cartel at the end of 2008.

Many OPEC nations, including Venezuela, which has the largest reserves of oil in the Western Hemisphere, have clearly stated their opposition to the West, and to American foreign policy in particular. Nevertheless, the United States remains dependent upon the major OPEC producers, which supply nearly 60 percent of the approximately 20 million barrels of oil a day it consumes.[46] The solution to depending on imports from OPEC and other sources would seem straightforward: produce more oil domestically, in the United States.

But this solution is not as straightforward as it seems—and production price is the obstacle. The cost of pumping oil—called the "lifting" price—in the Persian Gulf can be in the vicinity of $3 per barrel; in the Gulf of Mexico, where the oil is much deeper, the lifting cost can be as high as $35 per barrel.[47] So, oil from Saudi Arabia and many other locations is far cheaper than oil from places in the United States.

Demand for OPEC oil is expected to increase over the next 20 years, requiring OPEC's production to increase dramatically to keep up. Estimates suggest that a global investment of some $16 trillion in energy supplies may need to be made by 2030 to keep up with demand.[48] But many OPEC members are reluctant to accept foreign investment.

 ## BASKETS AND BLENDS

In order to set a price for crude oil, OPEC must collect price information on several different crude oils. This collection is called a "basket" of crude oils. This basket is used to calculate a mathematical average based on these different crude oils.

From January 1, 1987, to June 15, 2005, OPEC used seven different crude oils to create this basket: Algeria's Saharan Blend, Indonesia Minas, Nigeria Bonny Light, Saudi Arabia Arab Light, Dubai Fateh, Venezuela Tia Juana, and Mexico Isthmus (a non-OPEC oil). The price of this basket rose dramatically from the year 2000, when it cost $27.60 per barrel, to 2005, when it was $50.71 per barrel.

At a meeting on June 15, 2005, OPEC members decided to change the way they calculated the basket and the blends of crude oils that made up the basket, a decision OPEC stated was to "better reflect the average quality of crude oil in OPEC Member Countries."[49] As of June 16, 2005, then, OPEC began using a basket of 11 crude oils, representing the main export crudes of all its member countries. The crude oils represented now include Algeria's Saharan Blend, Indonesia Minas, Iran Heavy, Iraq Basra Light, Kuwait Export, Libya's Es Sider, Nigeria Bonny Light, Qatar Marine, Saudi Arabia Arab Light, Murban (United Arab Emirates), and BCF 17 (Venezuela).

HOW OPEC OPERATES

Thirteen nations currently form OPEC: Iran, Iraq, Kuwait, Saudi Arabia, Venezuela, Qatar, Indonesia, Libya, Ecuador, the United Arab Emirates, Algeria, Nigeria, and Angola. (With the withdrawal of Indonesia at the end of 2008, OPEC membership will be down to 12.) Each of these member countries has a representative—known as its "head of delegation," who may or may not be the oil or energy minister of that member country—who is designated to meet at OPEC conferences.

The purpose of these conferences is generally to coordinate oil policies with the goals of promoting a certain amount of stability in the oil market and protecting each member country's oil revenue. It is also the duty of the conference to decide whether to accept a country's application for membership in OPEC, to approve the members of the board of governors, and to elect the chairman of this board. Finally, the conference is charged with deciding upon OPEC's budget, which is submitted by the board of governors. Conferences are generally held twice a year, in March and September, though special meetings, known as extraordinary meetings, may also be called if necessary.

In addition to the heads of delegation, the OPEC structure consists of a board of governors and a secretary general who make up the OPEC Secretariat. Several boards and committees also operate within OPEC.

The board of governors operates much like a company's governing board or board of directors. The board oversees the day-to-day management of OPEC, making sure that any resolutions approved at a conference are acted upon, that OPEC's annual budget is drafted, and that appropriate reports and recommendations are submitted to the conference. Each member country nominates a "governor" to serve on the board.

The secretary general is the chief executive of the OPEC secretariat. He serves as the authorized representative of OPEC

(continues on page 72)

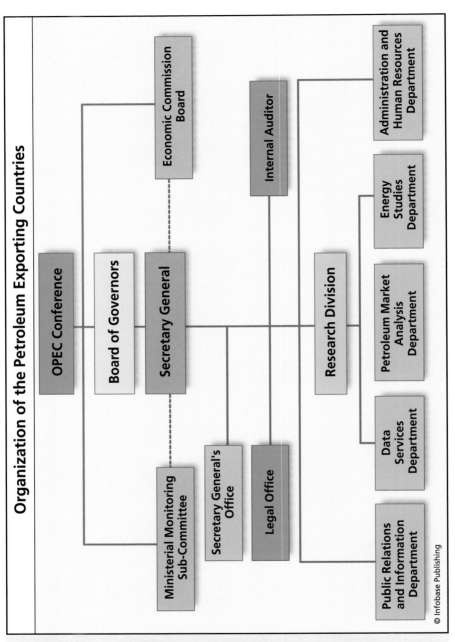

Organization of the Petroleum Exporting Countries

© Infobase Publishing

OPEC representatives meet regularly to discuss national policies and the international oil market. OPEC members also hold meetings throughout the levels of the organization, and within their own governments, in order to keep the oil market stable.

SECRETARY GENERAL OF OPEC

OPEC's legally authorized representative is the secretary general. It is the secretary general who often serves as the public face of OPEC, explaining its positions at press conferences and in meetings with world leaders.

OPEC appoints the secretary general to a three-year term. This term can then be renewed once for an additional three years. Member countries nominate candidates for this position; if the members cannot reach a unanimous decision about which nominee is best qualified to serve as secretary general, the post is then filled on a rotating basis for two-year terms.

According to Article 28 of the OPEC Statute, the secretary general must be at least 35 years old; must have a degree from a

(continues)

Abdalla El-Badri, the secretary-general of OPEC, arrives at the Ministry of Mines and Petroleum in Quito, Ecuador, on May 22, 2008, as part of a week-long meeting with members Venezuela and Ecuador.

(continued)

recognized university in law, economics, science, engineering, or business administration; and must have at least 15 years of experience, including at least 10 years in a position directly related to the oil industry and at least 5 years in "highly responsible executive or managerial positions." The secretary general must also be a native of one of the member countries.

The current secretary general of OPEC is Abdalla El-Badri. El-Badri was appointed in January 2007 and is a native of Libya. He studied in the United States (he has a degree in accounting and business administration from Florida Southern University), worked for the oil company Esso (now ExxonMobil), and led a Libyan oil company, as well as serving as Libya's energy minister and deputy prime minister. In 1994 he temporarily served as OPEC's secretary general for six months.

(continued from page 69)
and sits (with three heads of delegation) on the Ministerial Monitoring Sub-Committee (MMSC), which was established in February 1993 to monitor the oil production and exports of member countries.

All executive functions are carried out by the OPEC secretariat. Its staff is made up of a research division and such departments as petroleum market analysis and energy studies, which might carry out research into energy and economics, prepare reports on OPEC output, or organize lectures and meetings. Member countries finance the ongoing maintenance of the secretariat through equal contributions.

When it was first established, the OPEC secretariat was based in Geneva, Switzerland; however, in 1965, the headquarters was moved to Vienna, Austria.

OPEC AND THE PRICE OF OIL

At their twice-yearly meetings, the members of OPEC review the current market for petroleum and the forecasts for future supply and demand. They then determine whether to increase or decrease production based on this information. Member countries are expected to abide by these production quotas as set for them by OPEC. But the quotas are not static—they are periodically reviewed as markets change and events in the producing country or elsewhere in the world change.

Production quotas help contribute to the ability of OPEC to coordinate its response to the petroleum market. When the market changes, OPEC can adjust oil production. For example, if something would cause an increased demand for oil, say an event that prevented some oil-producing country from maintaining its output, OPEC can increase production elsewhere to prevent the sudden rise in price that would follow the real or perceived shortfall in supply. In the same way, if an excess supply of oil is present in the market, for example, if a winter is especially mild and less oil is required for heating homes, then prices of oil will begin to drop. OPEC can then decrease its oil production in response. (It is important to remember that OPEC's decisions are not binding on non-OPEC members who produce oil. Still, because OPEC's oil exports represent such a significant percentage of the oil traded in the world, its role on the oil market is equally significant.)

OPEC's pricing and production decisions are simply one piece of the puzzle that determines the price of oil—a large piece, admittedly, but other factors do figure into the final amount consumers ultimately pay to run their cars or to heat their homes. Namely, it is important to remember that the price

OPEC sets is for crude oil, *not* the refined, final product of gasoline, diesel fuel, or heating oil. The process of refining the crude oil into an end product adds additional costs. The shipping of crude oil to refining plants and elsewhere before it is even distributed to a final destination adds expenses that have to be recovered, also. Then, of course, taxes are often added. All of these components may dramatically raise the price at the point of purchase or use. This explains why prices, say for a tank of gasoline, vary so widely from one country to another, regardless of the price OPEC has set for crude oil.

The High
Price of Oil

THE CITIZENS OF THE MEMBER COUNTRIES OF OPEC HAVE all paid a high price for the discovery of oil in their land. A look at the list of OPEC member countries makes this point very clear: For the most part, OPEC nations are not countries noted for their democratic systems of government, nor are they known because their general populations enjoy a high standard of living. Quite the contrary ... the discovery of oil may bring untold wealth to a country, but most often it is a monarch, dictator, or other authoritarian regime that benefits from those riches. Seldom does that wealth reach those who need it most.

At a meeting in Riyadh, Saudi Arabia, from November 17 to 18, 2007, the heads of state of OPEC member countries officially recognized that they had an obligation "to raise the living standards of our peoples" and that "eradicating poverty should be the first and overriding global priority guiding local, regional, and international efforts."[50] But the reality of oil economics in each of the member countries has not allowed fulfillment of the promise in these lofty words. Even with oil income totaling billions of dollars, most countries still experience poverty, along with government corruption and authoritarian leadership.

IRAN

Iran is an Islamic state, with which the United States does not maintain diplomatic relations. It is governed by religious clerics and a president, Mahmoud Ahmadinejad, who has routinely denounced the United States. The events that led to this complicated relationship, in which each nation routinely figures in the other's image of global terror, have developed from connections that are based, to a significant extent, on oil.

The British first staked their claim to the oil fields in Iran (then known as Persia) when the commodity was discovered there in 1908 by the British adventurer William Knox D'Arcy. The discovery led to formation of the Anglo-Iranian Oil Company, which was formed when the shah (Iran's leader)— generously gave his British allies a 51 percent ownership in the company for 60 years. As World War I approached, the British also oversaw construction of a major oil refinery in Iran that would become one of the largest in the world.

The oil that should have been such a boom to the Iranian economy quickly became a source of discontent to the Iranian people. First of all, the Anglo-Iranian Oil Company refused to allow Iranians to audit its books to determine whether the company was providing a fair share of the oil revenue to the country's citizens. It seemed that Great Britain was benefiting more from Iranian oil than Iranians were. Mohammed Mossadeq, an Iranian politician, was determined to challenge this injustice. Mossadeq was opposed, first of all, to the control

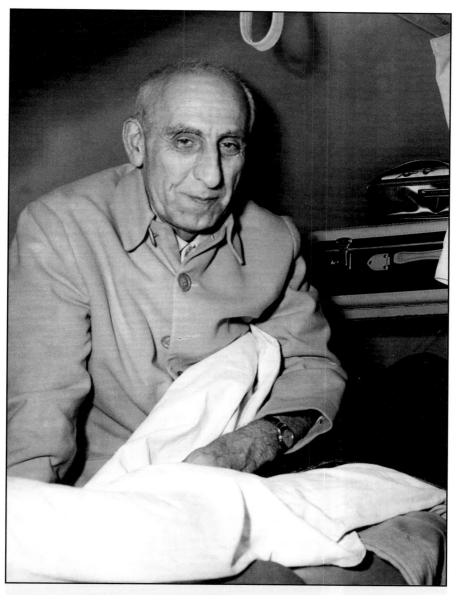

Ailing Iranian prime minister Mohammed Mossadeq traveled by plane
to The Hague in 1952 to contest the International Court's compe-
tence to rule in the Anglo-Iranian Oil Company case. When he became
prime minister of Iran, Mossadeq ordered all British employees of the
company out of Iran and nationalized the oil fields.

of Iranian oil by British oil company officials; he was, secondly, outraged at the excesses of the Iranian shah and at the ruler's willingness to barter away his country's resources for the purpose of further enhancing his personal wealth.

To begin his fight, Mossadeq called for the nationalization of Iran's oil fields, meaning that they would no longer belong to the Anglo-Iranian Oil Company or to the shah, but instead to the Iranian government. Mossadeq was supported in his efforts by Islamic clerics opposed to the British presence in Iran and to the corrupt policies of the shah. On April 29, 1951, Mossadeq was chosen by the Iranian parliament to serve as prime minister. He quickly ordered all British employees of the Anglo-Iranian Oil Company out of the country, leaving the oil fields in the hands of untrained Iranians, who lacked the expertise to operate the drilling wells or the company's refinery. In retaliation, the British government and its citizens boycotted Iranian oil. Without oil revenue, the economy of Iran began to collapse. With the shah in Rome, having fled the country with his family, Mossadeq turned to the United States for assistance and support. (For some time, the Soviets had threatened to "liberate" Iran from its corrupt shah; Mossadeq used this threat to form an alliance with the United States, to keep Communism from spreading into the Middle East.)

Instead, the United States worked behind the scenes to restore the shah to power, believing that he would be a better ally—that is, would be more favorable to American interests in regards to oil—than Mossadeq. Not only was the shah returned to his throne, but he was also equipped with American loans to help stabilize the economy, with programs to train Iranian oil workers, and with new markets for selling Iranian oil.

The revenues that followed generated even more wealth for the shah and his family. The shah built lavish palaces, hosted elaborate parties at which American politicians and leaders were frequent guests, and used American aid to build the kind of military that ensured Iran would become a powerful force in the Middle East. To protect himself from another Mossadeq, he established—with the help of the CIA—a secret police force that quickly became the most feared organization in Iran. Any left-over moneys were hidden in foreign banks outside Iran. But they also provided the shah's American allies with access to energy. Discontent spread and blossomed into revolution in 1979, when the shah was forced to leave the country and the American embassy was seized, along with several hostages—America's past support of the corrupt shah had not been forgotten.

For more than two decades, Iranian leaders demanded that the United States apologize for its role in overthrowing an elected government and returning a corrupt monarch to power. (Finally, on March 17, 2000, President Bill Clinton's Secretary of State, Madeleine Albright, gave a speech in Washington acknowledging America's role in Mossadeq's overthrow. "In 1953, the United States played a significant role in orchestrating the overthrow of Iran's popular prime minister, Mohammad Mossadeq," she said. "The Eisenhower administration believed its actions were justified for strategic reasons, but the coup was clearly a setback for Iran's political development. And it is easy to see now why many Iranians continue to resent this intervention by America in their internal affairs.")

Oil continues to play a critical, and unusual, role in Iran's economy, a country suffering from unemployment that some estimates suggest may be as high as 30 percent.[51] Because oil plays such a visible role in Iran's economy, the government provides oil at pennies per gallon (which helps suggest why gasoline consumption is rising by 10 percent a year and why massive traffic jams clog the streets of Iran's capital city, Tehran, with some three million cars.[52]) This gift of cheap oil to its people comes with a heavy price tag for the Iranian government because the country is now consuming more gasoline than its refineries can produce—Iran must export crude oil to foreign refineries, then pay to reimport gasoline. This cost the Iranian government $4.7 billion in 2004.[53]

In spite of this odd arrangement, few voices can challenge this poor management of oil because of Iran's authoritarian form of government. While Iran has an elected president and a parliament, a great deal of the power lies in the hands of a group of religious clerics, whose chief *ayatollah* serves as spokesman. These clerics run 58 percent of the Iranian budget through tax-exempt organizations called *bonyads*. These bonyads were initially intended to be charitable organizations, but over the years they have become closer to miniature businesses with social and religious influence. They use their power to provide jobs to supporters and punish their opponents.[54] The system supports corruption and oppression and helps explain why a nation can have vast oil revenues and yet have citizens who still suffer from unemployment and poverty.

NIGERIA

Nigeria became a member of OPEC in 1971. It currently exports some 2.5 billion barrels of oil a day—enough to make up 10 percent of U.S. oil imports and provide 80 percent of Nigeria's national income[55]—and still has vast oil resources waiting to be tapped. Oil was first extracted in Nigeria in 1957, and three years later the country gained independence from the United Kingdom. But for many of the years that followed—some 28 years in total—the country was under military rule. Civil war in 1967 resulted in the brutal slaughter of many Nigerians—ethnic tensions over control of the country's oil helped lead to that war.

In recent years, warlords have threatened Nigeria's oil industry, either by stealing crude oil directly from the pipelines or by using weapons and violence to seize control of oil-rich territory, particularly in the Niger Delta, where much of the country's oil resources are found. Alhaji Dokubo Asari is one such warlord. He is the leader of a powerful militia of roughly 3,000 well-armed men who steal crude oil directly from the pipelines and then sell it on the black market. Asari defends his actions as ultimately justified. "I take that which belongs

Here, a man looks at a stitched hole in a pipeline that exploded and killed 200 people who were trying to scoop fuel from it at Ilado beach village in Lagos, Nigeria, in May 2006. In recent years, warlords have threatened Nigeria's oil industry, either by vandalizing oil pipelines and stealing oil or by seizing control of oil-rich territory.

to me," he told Human Rights Watch. "It is not theft. The oil belongs to our people."[56]

(When oil is found in a town or village, it is seldom those who live closest to the discovery who benefit. Oil companies, most of them foreign, extract the oil and pay fees to the regional or national ruler. As just one example, during his five-year reign, from 1993 to 1998, Nigeria's former military dictator, Sani Abacha, allegedly received as much as $2.2 billion.[57])

In September 2004, Asari threatened to attack the Nigerian government and its oil companies; those threats were credible enough to spark a dramatic rise in the price of crude oil world-wide. (According to reporter Lisa Margonelli, such theft of oil and its resale on the black market is not a problem unique to Nigeria. In Colombia, right-wing militias steal 7,000 barrels of refined gasoline a day from pipelines. And armed gangs steal entire oil tankers off the coast of Somalia and near the Iraqi port of Basra—they then change the vessel's name or transfer its contents to another tanker nearby.[58])

 A LEGACY OF OIL

Nigerian author Ken Saro-Wiwa led many nonviolent protests against Shell and the Nigerian government. He fought to preserve Nigerian land for the ethnic Ogoni people who had lived on it for centuries, and he demanded greater political representation and accountability for environmental hazards created by oil extraction. He was ultimately arrested and executed. His son, Ken Wiwa, detailed his father's final hours in the book *In the Shadow of a Saint*, from which this excerpt is taken:

> He wanted to leave the world with a few words that would not only haunt his oppressors but also inspire future generations to continue the struggle. He rehearsed his last words, trying to imagine the most dramatic and appropriate moment to deliver them. As he considered the various scenarios, he was conscious of the need to guard against the numbing terror of that moment when he heard the clank of the key as the warden opened his cell to allow the soldiers stationed outside to lead him away to be executed. He didn't want to be surprised. He didn't want to react in a way that would betray any anxiety he might be feeling about dying. He

Foreign oil companies sometimes attempt to make local restitution by housing their workers in specially constructed quarters, with access to water and electricity that those in the nearby villages do not have. Development projects are heavily promoted, but often crippled by corruption or by a lack of training to make them operable. In 1992, Shell Oil Company built a schoolhouse in one Nigerian village; it is now closed and rotting. There were no teachers to staff the school, and no

realized that the way he reacted at that particular moment would set the tone for the rest of what remained of his life. He would stiffen his resolve, hold his head up high. He wanted history to record that he did not flinch when they came to take him away ...

[Late in the morning of November 10, 1995, he was led from his cell to be executed.] He straightened his back and shuffled defiantly into the hut that housed the gallows. A priest followed him ... then came out again. There was a short delay, then my father's voice echoed around the courtyard: "What sort of country is this that delights in the killing of its illustrious citizens? What have I done that I deserve death, than that I spoke the truth, demanding justice for my poor people of Ogoni? I have always been a man of good ideas, and whether I be killed, my ideas will live forever, and Ogoni, for which I am dying, will one day be emancipated from the shackles of oppression."*

---

* Ken Wiwa, *In the Shadow of a Saint: A Son's Journey to Understand His Father's Legacy.* South Royalton, VT: Steerforth Press, 2001.

program to train or develop them.[59] Such gifts, as well as those of a hospital or water treatment plant, are of little use without the workers to operate them.

In Nigeria, the government has gone so far as to claim any land that contains oil, as well as the oil itself. A protest organization formed by Nigerian activist Ken Saro-Wiwa was designed to fight to preserve land for the ethnic groups that had inhabited it. The organization also demanded greater political representation and specifically targeted Shell Oil Company for its role in contaminating the environment through oil spills. Using nonviolent protests, Saro-Wiwa's group was able to shut down certain Shell facilities. The Nigerian military ultimately intervened, however, occupying much of the region and arresting Saro-Wiwa and eight other members of his group. Saro-Wiwa and the others were falsely accused of murder and executed on November 10, 1995, despite a huge international outcry against the sentence.

Violence and corruption cripple the oil industry in Nigeria, illustrating the need for a new kind of oil diplomacy, one that factors in development and peacekeeping, as well as basic human rights for the citizens of the oil-producing nation. Thus far, these factors have played little role in OPEC negotiations.

VENEZUELA

It was a Venezuelan, Juan Pablo Pérez Alfonso, who played a key role in the founding of OPEC; today, under the leadership of President Hugo Chávez, Venezuela has been taking steps to increase its present-day influence in the organization.[60] Chávez has championed the creation of an "OPEC university" that would specialize in research and developing new technology for the oil industry. He has also argued to expand OPEC membership to include countries like Russia, Mexico, and Norway.

Oil makes up half of Venezuela's income. As the largest oil producer in the Western Hemisphere, Venezuela is naturally an important supplier of oil to the United States—in fact, some

70 percent of all Venezuelan oil is sold to the United States.[61] But the relationship is complicated, made more so by the U.S. endorsement of a short-lived coup in 2002 that removed Chávez from power for a mere two days—and also dissolved the legislative and judicial branches of the Venezuelan government.

Chávez is strongly supported by the Venezuelan poor, despite the fact that few of them have benefited from Venezuelan oil riches—the Venezuelan national oil company, PDVSA, has an income of $42 billion, but more than half of Venezuela's population lives on less than $2 a day.[62]

Oil was discovered in Venezuela in 1921 and, according to the law then in place, belonged to the farmers who owned the land on which it was discovered. Unfortunately for them, U.S. oil companies preferred to negotiate with a single government figure, particularly one who would be friendly to their interests, rather than a complicated network of independent farmers. Then-dictator Juan Vicente Gómez (whom the United States had helped bring to power) was willing to cooperate, and he quickly announced that the land, and any oil it contained, belonged to the Venezuelan government.

What followed was a series of corrupt regimes, often supported quietly by the United States, who allowed the disparity between the "haves" and "have-nots" to grow ever greater. Oil brought tremendous wealth to the country, money that its leaders spent lavishly and often foolishly. Much of it was spent rushing to "modernize" the country by building a vast network of highways, luxurious apartment buildings, a modern university, and even a mountaintop ice rink.[63] As happened elsewhere, Venezuelans left their farms and villages and moved into the cities, seeking greater opportunity and the promise of wealth. And, as happened elsewhere, the country was gradually forced to rely more and more on imports.

The Venezuelan government continued to spend money; even when oil prices fell in the 1980s, the government did not reduce its spending. Instead, it borrowed money, using its oil

Larry Chretien, executive director of Mass Energy; Felix Rodriguez, chief executive officer of Citgo; Representative Bill Delahunt; and Joseph Kennedy, chairman and founder of Citizens Energy Corporation pulled a fuel hose to a house during a November 2005 ceremony in Quincy, Mass. Citgo, a subsidiary of Petroleos de Venezuela, S.A., provides heavily discounted oil to needy families in the United States.

reserves as collateral. The national debt grew and prices for food, utilities, and other products were all raised in an effort to stop the country from sinking further into debt. Chávez came to power promising to end the period of corruption. He assured the masses that ordinary Venezuelans would benefit from the country's valuable oil resources.

Despite his frequent rhetoric against the West, only a select group of impoverished Americans have benefited from Chávez's brand of oil diplomacy. (Citizen Energy, a nonprofit organization that works through the oil company Citgo—Citgo is a petroleum company in which Venezuela owns a controlling share—provides million of gallons of heating oil to more than 400,000 low-income households in 16 American states.[64]) His own people still struggle to reap benefits from their own valuable resource, although Chávez has improved access to healthcare in some of Venezuela's more remote regions, developed a program to increase literacy, and discounted the costs of some basic foods, including frozen chickens, dehydrated milk, and rice.

Like many OPEC nations, Venezuela now faces a dilemma. Money needs to be invested in the oil fields to upgrade equipment and ensure continued productivity. But many foreign investors are wary of investing in countries wracked by violence or political instability, or governments where anti-Western speech is particularly fierce. Venezuela and other nations facing this dilemma must either find a national source for the money to invest in upgrading their wells and equipment or allow their fields to become less productive, less profitable, and less important.

THE CYCLE OF OIL

As these case histories show, the arrival of oil in a country is seldom the solution to a nation's economic struggles—or, more accurately, it is seldom a solution to the poverty and unemployment of its people. Instead, it more often leads to corruption, violence, and dictatorial forms of government, and continued poverty and unemployment.

The cycle is clear. Sudden, vast wealth from oil enables a government to replace other forms of financial support with oil money. Exports frequently are sacrificed—exports other than oil, that is—forcing the nation to begin to import products like food and other essentials for daily life. With oil revenues funding the government, the need for taxing ordinary citizens falls to the wayside. However, this seldom proves beneficial to the people of an oil-exporting nation. Raising money from taxes usually requires winning the people's consent to them, often through a representative body. Without a representative body, there are few ways to ensure that oil revenue or other burdens and benefits are fairly distributed in a society. Inevitably, a few benefit while the vast majority are left in poverty.

Oil inspires envy from within and without. Governments begin to spend more and more of their oil revenue on building militaries and militias to defend against external threats and to ensure that they remain in power. One World Bank study has shown that oil-rich nations are 40 percent more likely to fall into civil war than nations that don't have significant oil resources.[65] Other studies have shown that countries whose economy is dominated by oil exports tend to experience shrinking standards of living, and that developing countries without oil grew four times as much as those with oil.[66]

There are other cases, of course.

When oil was discovered in the United States, in Canada, in Norway, and in the United Kingdom, for example, it was extracted without creating or expanding an authoritarian government, without creating crippling instances of corruption, and without opening chasms between the rich few and the many poor. But, in these cases, the countries involved had established, democratic systems of government in place *before* oil was discovered, as well as economies that were solid and diversified, where oil could serve as an additional—rather than a dominant—source of revenue.[67]

OPEC on the
World Stage

FOR THE PAST 30 YEARS, OPEC HAS PLAYED AN IMPORTANT role in global politics, using access to oil as a tool to influence policy and impact economic development. OPEC members currently hold about three-fourths of the world's proven oil reserves, and will likely continue to supply oil to much of the world for the next several decades.

In its control over such a significant percentage of the world's proven oil reserves; in its ability to regulate production and set prices; and in its willingness to use oil as a political weapon to shape policy, OPEC has proven its ability to dramatically impact the global economy. One noteworthy example is the 1970s oil embargo, when OPEC triggered gasoline shortages throughout the United States.

Still, OPEC's power was challenged in the 1980s, when—especially in the United States—an emphasis was placed on improving fuel economy and finding non-OPEC sources of oil. But OPEC remains the leading supplier of the cheapest, most easily accessible oil, and as such its power to influence the economies of developed countries remains strong. (Non-OPEC oil production is expected to rise slightly in the near future, as well, but not enough to keep pace with total world oil demand.[68])

In recent years, the economies of developing countries in Asia, especially China and India, have become increasingly oil-dependent. The rapid pace of development there and the vast number of potential consumers suggest that demand for oil will become even greater, increasing OPEC's influence even more. In all, more than 200 countries and territories are not members of OPEC, and 85 percent of these were oil importers in 2004.[69] Even countries that produce their own oil—like the United States—need additional sources of oil to supplement what they can produce nationally.

The effort to locate and develop new sources of oil brings its own challenges and responsibilities. When oil is discovered on their land, developing countries frequently see their fragile governments dissolve into violence and result in dictatorship. Seldom do the people of those countries benefit from the resource discovered in their land. Corruption is rampant. Civil war is a constant threat. Nations that manage to hold together and become major oil producers quickly become dependent on oil revenue for economic survival. OPEC members can boast of vast revenues, but the wealth is almost always held in the hands of a select group of businessmen and government leaders.

REDUCING OPEC'S INFLUENCE

As long as oil remains a critical element of industrial development and global economies, OPEC will remain a highly influential member of the international community. Efforts to reduce that influence rely primarily on two possibilities: finding alternate sources of oil and reducing dependence on oil. These approaches are not revolutionary or unexplored. As we have seen, a combination of the two was enacted in the United States, following OPEC's 1973 oil embargo, with some success.

Currently, OPEC only supplies about 40 percent of the world's oil; but much of the other 60 percent will become increasingly expensive to tap, making it difficult for producers of these sources to comply with or compete with OPEC pricing. Geologist Colin J. Campbell blames OPEC members for creating the idea that they control a limitless supply of oil by implying that "they could flood the world with cheap oil at the flick of a switch," thereby decreasing any incentive to study alternatives like natural gas, renewable energy sources, or conservation of oil.[70] But Campbell and other experts go on to suggest that the reality is actually far grimmer—that the United States, Europe, and other developing economies will become even more increasingly dependent on foreign sources of oil, forcing them to support unstable, undemocratic, and even unjust regimes in order to ensure their flow of energy.

Given the choices, replacing oil with other sources of energy, as well as adopting new habits of fuel efficiency and conservation, will go the farthest in helping stem OPEC's influence. According to Michael T. Klare, author of *Blood and Oil: The Dangers of America's Growing Petroleum Dependency*, the United States consumes approximately 20 million barrels of oil a day, or about 840 million gallons. Roughly 70 percent of that amount is used for transportation—cars, trucks, buses, and other motor vehicles.[71] This major slice of the consumption pie could be reduced through simple conservation strategies. According to the International Energy Agency:

- reducing the highway speed limit to 50 mph could save 738,000 barrels of oil a day;

Gasoline prices hit a record high in 2008, causing commuters to abandon their cars and join the millions of people who use public transportation. Subways, buses, and trains have experienced an increase in ridership as the economy and the environment become increasingly important concerns for consumers. *Above*, the Bay Area Rapid Transit System (BART) in San Francisco, California.

- building a workable carpooling system could save 770,000 barrels a day;
- promoting telecommuting could save 538,000 barrels a day;
- inflating tires to proper levels could save 154,000 barrels a day; and
- passing laws to increase the fuel efficiency regulations for cars would save 2.5 million barrels a day by 2015.

Any combination of these simple conservation strategies would save millions of barrels of oil each day—and reduce

OPEC's ability to shape foreign policy by threatening to turn off the tap.[72]

A LOOK AHEAD

From the time of its creation in 1960, OPEC has focused on its core mission of securing a steady income for oil-producing nations. Influenced by unfair relationships with foreign governments and oil companies that seized their valuable local resource, the members of OPEC devoted efforts in the early years to defending themselves and obtaining the most favorable relationships for themselves with foreign oil companies. Initially, this involved getting a greater percentage of profits from the oil companies and more involvement with the process of drilling and extracting the oil. Later, OPEC's influence grew to controlling the price of oil and limiting production quotas.

Today, OPEC's stated mission is

> to ensure the stabilization of oil prices in international oil markets with a view to eliminating harmful and unnecessary fluctuations, due regard being given at all times to the interests of oil-producing nations and to the necessity of securing a steady income for them; an efficient, economic and regular supply of petroleum to consuming nations; and a fair return on capital to those investing in the petroleum industry.[73]

But the reality of carrying out this mission is far more complicated than it sounds because the goals may come in conflict with each other when the interests of oil-producing nations come in conflict with those of oil-consuming nations. In those cases, OPEC has demonstrated that its focus will be on protecting the income of oil-producing nations first.

In addition, OPEC has demonstrated that its mandate will extend beyond economic goals. In 1973, the oil embargo by OPEC was used to penalize nations that had supported Israel in the Arab-Israeli War in the Middle East. More recently, OPEC nations have refused to increase oil production to compensate for increased demand from China or rising oil prices in the United States.

It seems clear that OPEC will remain a powerful political force in the near future, and that its member nations will continue to influence the pace and extent of economic development in many countries. Each member has its own distinct culture and each has experienced its own dramatic transformation since the discovery of oil within its borders. But in moving forward, it will be each member's ability to set aside its differences and to cooperate within the framework of OPEC to achieve certain specific goals that will contribute to OPEC's strengthening position in shaping the global economy.

1960   Representatives from Iran, Iraq, Kuwait, Saudi Arabia, and Venezuela meet in Baghdad, Iraq, to form OPEC.

1961   Qatar joins OPEC. Iraq leaves OPEC temporarily to protest Kuwaiti land squabble.

1962   Libya and Indonesia join OPEC.

1965   OPEC moves headquarters from Geneva, Switzerland, to Vienna, Austria.

1967   United Arab Emirates joins OPEC. Arab-Israeli War leads Arab oil ministers to call for an oil embargo against countries who are friendly to Israel and results in closure of the Suez Canal. In addition, civil war breaks out in Nigeria. These events begin to transform global oil markets and establish OPEC as a force in the industry.

1969   Algeria joins OPEC. Revolution in Libya brings Colonel Muammar Qaddafi to power and opens the way to introduction of the "Libyan Method" of negotiating oil rights.

1971   Nigeria joins OPEC.

1973   OPEC demonstrates its newfound clout by raising prices and establishing an oil embargo against nations thought to be friendly to Israel. Gasoline shortages and rationing methods rock U.S. consumers.

1974   OPEC oil shipments to the United States resume in the spring after showing the world that the organization *can* control prices and availability. This is the beginning of OPEC's Golden Age.

1975   U.S. Congress passes the Energy Policy and Conservation Act and creates the Strategic Petroleum

Reserve, both to help thwart future OPEC actions against the United States.

1978   OPEC's Golden Age ends after a $67 billion surplus is wasted into a $2 billion deficit. Civil unrest in Iran leads to a global panic and efforts to stockpile oil.

1988   OPEC votes to drop the fixed-price system that had been in place since the group's inception; crude oil prices will now be set by international market conditions, supply and demand.

1990   Iraq invades Kuwait and other OPEC members increase production to compensate for lost revenues from the two warring countries.

1992   Ecuador suspends membership.

1995   Gabon withdraws from membership.

2007   Angola joins OPEC; Ecuador rejoins.

2008   Indonesia decides to withdraw from OPEC at the end of the year.

NOTES

Introduction

1. Benjamin Shwadran, *Middle East Oil Crises Since 1973*. Boulder, CO: Westview Press, 1986, 2.
2. Rachel Bronson, *Thicker than Oil: America's Uneasy Partnership with Saudi Arabia*. New York: Oxford University Press, 2006, 82.
3. Ibid., 81.
4. "What is OPEC?" Available online. URL: http://www.opec.org/library/FAQs/aboutOPEC/q1.htm.

Chapter 1

5. Matthew Yeomans, *Oil: Anatomy of an Industry*. New York: The New Press, 2004, xii–xiii.
6. Ibid., xi.
7. Lisa Margonelli, *Oil on the Brain: Adventures from the Pump to the Pipeline*. New York: Doubleday, 2007, 221.
8. Ibid., 50.
9. Ibid., 59.

Chapter 2

10. Daniel Yergin, *The Prize*. New York: Simon & Schuster, 1991, 523.
11. Ibid., 524.
12. Mohammed E. Ahrari, *OPEC*. Lexington, KY: University Press of Kentucky, 1986, 24.
13. Yergin, *The Prize*, 528.
14. Ahrari, *OPEC*, 28.
15. Ibid., 33.
16. Ibid., 34.
17. Yergin, *The Prize*, 541.
18. Ibid., 542.

Chapter 3

19. Yeomans, *Anatomy of an Industry*, xviii.
20. Yergin, *The Prize*, 583.
21. Ibid., 584.
22. Ibid., 585.
23. Ibid., 598.
24. Ibid., 602.
25. Ibid., 607.
26. Yeomans, *Anatomy of an Industry*, 25–26.
27. Margonelli, *Oil on the Brain*, 105.
28. Ibid., 106.
29. Ibid., 111.
30. Ibid., 114.
31. Samuel W. Bodman, "Statement on the Expansion of the Strategic Petroleum Reserve to 1.5 Billion," U.S. Department of Energy Office of Public Affairs, January 23, 2007. Available online. URL: http://www.energyinnovator.com/index.php?articleID=10106&sectionID=119.

Chapter 4

32. Yergin, *The Prize*, 634.
33. Ibid., 625.
34. Ibid., 634.
35. Ibid., 635.
36. C.J. Campbell, *Oil Crisis*. Essex, UK: Multi-Science Publishing, 2005, 247.
37. Yergin, *The Prize*, 687.
38. Ibid., 718.
39. Fadhil J. Al-Chalabi, "The World Oil Price Collapse of 1986: Causes and Implications for the Future of OPEC," in Wilfrid L. Kohl (ed.), *After the Oil Price Collapse: OPEC, the United States, and the World Market*. Baltimore, MD: The Johns Hopkins University Press, 1991, 4.

40. Ibid., 9.
41. Yergin, *The Prize*, 750.

Chapter 5
42. Yergin, *The Prize*, 773.
43. Margonelli, *Oil on the Brain*, 135.

Chapter 6
44. EIA Country Analysis Briefs, "OPEC." Available online.
     URL: http://www.eia.doe.gov/cabs/opec.html.
45. Margonelli, *Oil on the Brain*, 130.
46. Ibid., 5.
47. Ibid., 97.
48. Ibid., 144.
49. EIA Country Analysis Briefs, "OPEC."

Chapter 7
50. "Riyadh Declaration: The Third Summit of Heads of
     State and Government of OPEC Member Countries,"
     Riyadh, Kingdom of Saudi Arabia, November 17–18,
     2007. Available online. URL: http://www.opec.org/about
     us/III%20OPEC%20Summit%20Declaration.pdf.
51. Margonelli, *Oil on the Brain*, 211.
52. Ibid.
53. Ibid., 213.
54. Ibid.
55. Ibid., 235.
56. Ibid., 238.
57. Ibid., 239.
58. Ibid., 241.
59. Yeomans, *Anatomy of an Industry*, 81.
60. Christina Hoag, "Will OPEC Go Along with Chavez's
     Ambitions?" *Business Week*, October 2, 2000,
     www.businessweek.com/2000/00_40/b3701185.htm.

61.   Margonelli, *Oil on the Brain*, 139.

62.   Ibid., 138.

63.   Ibid., 145.

64.   Liza Featherstone, "Chavez's Citizen Diplomacy." *The Nation*, January 1, 2007, www.thenation.com/doc/ 20070101/featherstonev.

65.   Yeomans, *Anatomy of an Industry*, 83.

66.   Margonelli, *Oil on the Brain*, 175.

67.   Yeomans, *Anatomy of an Industry*, 66.

Chapter 8

68.   EIA Country Analysis Briefs, "Non-OPEC Fact Sheet," June 2005. Available online. URL: http://www.eia.doe. gov/emeu/cabs/nonopec.html.

69.   Ibid.

70.   Colin J. Campbell, "A Worldwide Oil Shortage Is Approaching," in Andrea C. Nakaya (ed.), *Oil*. Farmington Hills, MI: Greenhaven Press, 2006, 24.

71.   Michael T. Klare, "The United States Should Reduce its Consumption of Foreign Oil," in Andrea C. Nakaya (ed.), *Oil*. Farmington Hills, MI: Greenhaven Press, 2006, 113.

72.   Margonelli, *Oil on the Brain*, 115.

73.   OPEC, "What is OPEC?"

BIBLIOGRAPHY

Ahrari, Mohammed E. *OPEC: The Failing Giant.* Lexington, KY: The University Press of Kentucky, 1986.

Anderson, Irvine H. *Aramco, the United States, and Saudi Arabia: A Study of the Dynamics of Foreign Oil Policy, 1933–1950.* Princeton, NJ: Princeton University Press, 1981.

Bahgat, Gawdat. *American Oil Diplomacy in the Persian Gulf and the Caspian Sea.* Gainesville, FL: University Press of Florida, 2003.

Blair, John M. *The Control of Oil.* New York: Pantheon Books, 1976.

Bronson, Rachel. *Thicker than Oil: America's Uneasy Partnership with Saudi Arabia.* New York: Oxford University Press, 2006.

Campbell, C.J. *Oil Crisis.* Essex, UK: Multi-Science Publishing, 2005.

Gordon, Joy. "UN Oil for Food 'Scandal.'" *The Nation*, December 6, 2004. Available online. URL: http://www.thenation.com.

Jones, Bart. *Hugo.* Hanover, NH: Steerforth Press, 2007.

Kohl, Wilfrid L., ed. *After the Oil Price Collapse: OPEC, the United States, and the World Oil Market.* Baltimore, MD: The Johns Hopkins University Press, 1991.

Margonelli, Lisa. *Oil on the Brain: Adventures from the Pump to the Pipeline.* New York: Doubleday, 2007.

Nakaya, Andrea C., ed. *Oil.* Farmington Hills, MI: Greenhaven Press, 2006.

Shwadran, Benjamin. *Middle East Oil Crises Since 1973.* Boulder, CO: Westview Press, 1986.

Vernon, Raymond, ed. *The Oil Crisis.* New York: W.W. Norton & Company, 1976.

Wiwa, Ken. *In the Shadow of a Saint: A Son's Journey to Understand His Father's Legacy*. South Royalton, VT: Steerforth Press, 2001.

Yeomans, Matthew. *Oil: Anatomy of an Industry*. New York: The New Press, 2004.

Yergin, Daniel. *The Prize: The Epic Quest for Oil, Money, and Power*. New York: Simon & Schuster, 1991.

WEB SITES

Business Week
  http://www.businessweek.com.

Cable News Network
  http://www.cnn.com.

Energy Information Administration,
  U.S. Department of Energy
  http://www.eia.doe.gov.

U.S. Department of Energy
  http://www.energy.gov.

The *New York Times*
  http://www.nytimes.com.

Organization of the Petroleum Exporting Countries
  http://www.opec.org.

United States Department of Energy
  Strategic Petroleum Reserve Project
  http://www.spr.doe.gov.

The Nation
  http://www.thenation.com.

United Nations
  http://www.un.org.

FURTHER READING

Falola, Toyin, and Genova, Ann. *The Politics of the Global Oil Industry*. Westport, CT: Praeger Publishers, 2005.

Margonelli, Lisa. *Oil on the Brain: Adventures from the Pump to the Pipeline*. New York: Doubleday, 2007.

Parra, Francisco. *Oil Politics: A Modern History of Petroleum*. New York: I. B. Tauris, 2004.

Roberts, Paul. *The End of Oil*. New York: Mariner Books, 2005.

Yeomans, Matthew. *Oil: Anatomy of an Industry*. New York: The New Press, 2004.

Yergin, Daniel. *The Prize: The Epic Quest for Oil, Money, and Power*. New York: Free Press, 1993.

WEB SITES

Energy Information Administration:
  Official energy statistics from the U.S. government
  http://www.eia.doe.gov.

OPEC
  http://www.opec.org

World News Network: OPEC news
  http://www.opecnews.com.

PICTURE CREDITS

INDEX

Author **HEATHER LEHR WAGNER** has written extensively on the Middle East and international politics. Most recently, she authored new editions of *Iraq*, *Iran*, *Turkey*, and *Saudi Arabia*, all titles in the Creation of the Modern Middle East series. She earned a B.A. in political science from Duke University and an M.A. in government from the College of William and Mary. She lives with her family in Pennsylvania.

Series editor **PEGGY KAHN** is a professor of political science at the University of Michigan-Flint, where she teaches world and European politics. She has been a social studies volunteer in the Ann Arbor, Michigan, public schools, and she helps prepare college students to become teachers. She has a Ph.D. in political science from the University of California, Berkeley, and a B.A. in history and government from Oberlin College.